LONDON
Claiming the Future

Produced in cooperation with the
London Chamber of Commerce

London
CANADA

The London Area Chamber of Commerce and Community Communications, Inc.,
would like to express our gratitude to these companies for their leadership in the development of this book.

LONDON

Claiming the Future

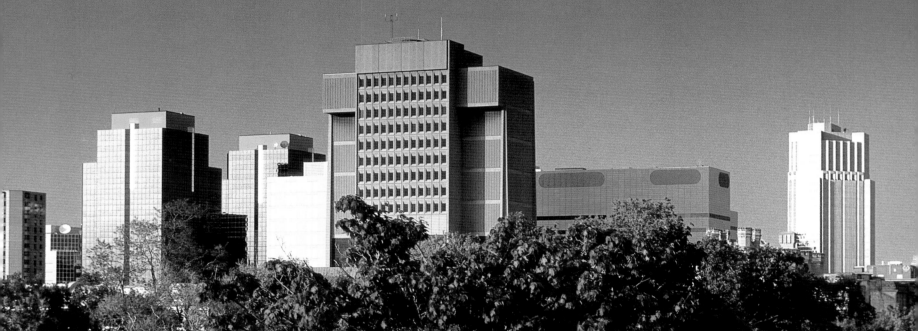

TABLE OF CONTENTS

LONDON

Claiming the Future

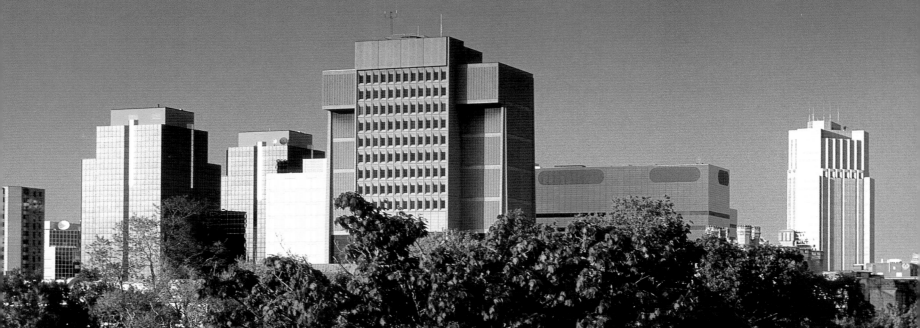

TABLE OF CONTENTS

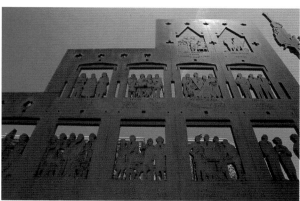

LONDON
Claiming the Future

By **Pat Morden**
Corporate Profiles by **Jim Etherington**
Featuring the photography of **Mike Grandmaison**

Community Communications, Inc.
Publisher: Ronald P. Beers

Staff for *London: Claiming the Future*

Acquisitions	**Henry S. Beers**
Publisher's Sales Associate	**Brian Rhodes, Greg Thain**
Editor in Chief	**Wendi Lewis**
Managing Editor	**Kurt R. Niland**
Profile Editor	**Amanda J. Burbank**
Design Director	**Scott Phillips**
Designer	**Eddie Lavoie**
Photo Editors	**Kurt R. Niland and Eddie Lavoie**
Proofreader	**Kari Collin Jarnot, Heather Edwards**
Editorial Assistant	**Rebekah Monson**
Contract Manager	**Christi Stevens**
Print Production Manager	**Jarrod Stiff**
Pre-Press and Separations	**Artcraft Graphic Productions**
National Sales Manager	**Ronald P. Beers**
Sales Assistant	**Sandra Akers**
Acquisitions Coordinator	**Angela P. White**
Accounting Services	**Stephanie Perez**

CCI

Community Communications, Inc.
Montgomery, Alabama

David M. Williamson, Chief Executive Officer
Ronald P. Beers, President
W. David Brown, Chief Operating Officer

FOREWORD

A quality, culturally diverse family environment; a winning spirit and an ideal home for business. That's London.

On behalf of the London Chamber of Commerce and its local businesses, we present this book to the London community.

Within these beautiful pages, it is our sincere hope that you will experience the quality, texture and healthy pulse of this dynamic city. We are rich in wonderful people, progressive partnerships and exciting opportunities. As you enjoy this book, you will come to understand why our future is so bright.

With the beginning of the new millennium, it's an exciting time in London. Those of us who live here know and appreciate the warmth and friendliness of our people, respect our traditions and heritage and look forward to many opportunities for a prosperous future.

We are proud to share with you a glimpse into the heart and soul of London, a city poised for remarkabke successes in the new millennium and, more simply, a great place to live, work, and do business. Most of all, however, London is a place simply to enjoy.

—*The London Chamber of Commerce*

PREFACE

Imagine appropriating the name of one of the world's great cities for a tiny Canadian frontier town. Calling stump-filled residential streets after the grand English thoroughfares of Piccadilly Street, Oxford Street and Pall Mall. Naming a muddy stream flowing through farmers' fields after the majestic Thames.

It was silly, really. Still, I find the pretensions of our Victorian founding fathers rather endearing. They had big dreams. They knew they lived somewhere special—somewhere that was destined to grow and prosper. They would be proud to see what their London has become. It is a vibrant, exciting city and a very special place to live and work. That's why it has been such an honor and delight to write this book—to stand back and look at my home with new eyes.

I am deeply grateful to the London Chamber of Commerce and Community Communications, Inc. for affording me this opportunity. My special thanks to all those in companies and organizations throughout London who assisted me with the research. And of course, thanks to Mike Grandmaison for his marvelous images.

My work on this book is dedicated to my husband, Max Morden. Max was a wonderful research assistant and helped me develop and shape each chapter. He was, and continues to be, my biggest cheerleader and my partner in every sense of the word.

—*Pat Morden*

part one

CHAPTER

O N E

London: A Personal Collage

I always feel a little embarrassed admitting that I have lived, and lived contentedly, in London nearly all my life.

After all, it is not too large a city. It has no mountains or oceans, and no man-made wonders. The surrounding countryside is fertile but unspectacular. The business community is diverse and successful, but there is no Bill Gates or George Soros. Am I simply too timid and unadventurous to live anywhere else?

Photo by Mike Grandmaison

Perhaps, but at the same time, London has a quiet charm that also works its magic on newcomers and returning natives. Like the land that surrounds it, it has a subtle beauty and provides rich soil for growth.

In some ways, it's London's ordinariness that is so heartwarming. It's a modest city, one unused to blowing its own horn. There's nothing to live up to, no need to be chic or savvy, no fashion parade to stay in step with. London is a place where any delay is considered a traffic jam, where, as a transplanted Maritimer once pointed out to me in disgust, people sweep the sidewalks in front of their houses to keep them tidy. It is comfortable, convenient and friendly.

At the same time, there is a seriousness about London. Londoners don't take their city for granted. They are concerned for it and want to see it succeed. And it's quite extraordinary how soon newcomers are converted from slightly superior observers to enthusiastic cheerleaders or reforming critics. Recently, a lively debate about London's future has engaged a wide range of people, diverse in opinion but united in their commitment to the city.

My personal image of London is a collage of snapshots taken from the time I was a few years old until recently. As my personal world expanded, new aspects of the city came into focus. Its growth has mirrored my own.

As a child I lived on a quiet, unpaved road in the northeast corner of what was then London. Now considered almost central, our street ended in a footbridge over a tiny creek, and farmland ran down to the backyards.

Some of my earliest memories are of Gibbon's Park, a riverside green space where I took swimming lessons in a frigid outdoor pool. Our church picnics were held in the park. The highlight, after three-legged and spoon races, was eating tiny tubs of vanilla ice cream with a flat wooden spoon.

When the weather grew cool and crisp, a trip to the market was always considered a treat. The air was filled with the tang of fresh apples and the warm, comforting aroma of baking bread and chickens on the barbecue. London is now famous for its proliferation of doughnut stores, but I tasted my first one at a stall on the market, and was enraptured by the combination of soft yeasty cake and thick chocolate icing.

At Christmas, we made the trip downtown to see the Santa Claus parade and admire the competing animated window displays at Simpson's and Eaton's. Then it was on to Victoria Park, transformed for the season with a dazzling display of colored lights. Once, when I was waiting for a bus on a bitter, damp day just before Christmas, a heart-lifting vision came into view—one of our familiar "peanut butter" buses had been transformed for the season with colorful painted scenes and lights. (The Christmas bus, I am glad to report, is still a London tradition.)

Because my father was a professor, the University of Western Ontario was always a part of my life. When I went with my mother to pick him up at the old Physics building, I had no idea that the ivy

City of London

The City of London is a vibrant centre of economic growth in southwestern Ontario, with a special focus on manufacturing, medical care and education. Known as the Forest City and also for its delightful parks and riverbank walkways along the Thames River. London is a desired community in which to live and work.

Served by the Greater London International Airport and a major railway system, London is ideally located at the intersection of highways 401 and 402, part of the North American Free Trade Superhighway links. The city is surrounded by the most productive agricultural land in Canada and has been a historical Ontario centre for almost two centuries.

Photo by Mike Grandmaison

London Health Sciences Centre

London Health Sciences Centre is one of Canada's largest teaching hospitals. The year 2000 marks the 125th anniversary of this merged organization's provision of health care to the London community and the 5th anniversary of newly merged London Health Sciences Centre (formerly University and Victoria Hospitals). The primary commitment of LHSC is to excellence in patient care, with a number of its clinical programs achieving provincial and in some cases national and international recognition. To ensure excellence in health care for future generations of patients, London Health Sciences Centre is also dedicated to providing high quality teaching, and to the advancement of scientific knowledge through research. Renowned not only across Canada but around the world, London Health Sciences Centre is a major contributor to the city's historic role as a leader in patient care, teaching and research.

covering the walls concealed exquisite little gargoyles carved by skilled stonemasons early in this century. Nor did I sense the immense ferment of intellectual activity that has made Western one of Canada's leading universities.

Stage-struck from an early age, I took acting lessons at the Grand Theatre, revelling in its ramshackle, vaudeville-era splendor. The theatre is now beautifully renovated and houses an excellent professional theatre company. As teenagers, my friends and I began to spend our Saturday afternoons at London's first shopping mall, the oh-so-modern Wellington Square Mall, which presaged the city's rapid growth as a retail centre.

By the time I was 16, we, like so many families, had moved to the 'burbs. Our street, a barren farmer's field dotted with almost identical houses when we moved in, is now a mature and shady avenue. The first McDonald's in Eastern Canada opened a few blocks from my high school and soon became a regular stop. When friends began to drive, we discovered pleasures just beyond the city—the Komoka gravel pits or the Pinery beach for swimming, the theatres at Stratford (cheap rush seats) for entertainment. Springbank Park, home of the beloved Slippery the Seal in my childhood, became a conveniently dark and romantic spot to stop a car late at night.

When it was time for university, I learned my way around a substantially expanded campus and spent many hours in the concrete caverns of the Weldon Library. A history student and later an employee of the university archives room, I began to develop an interest in the city's history and its colorful characters.

The city, meanwhile, was growing around me, expanding in all directions, but particularly to the south and west. Suburbs and

Hilton London Ontario

The 322-room, Four Diamond Hilton London is a downtown landmark, a preeminent community meeting and conference centre, and a favourite dining and entertainment destination. Ideally located and connected by a walkway to the London Convention Centre, Hilton London is a convenient base for guests to explore nearby entertainment spots in the city's historic downtown, walk to London's treasured Grand Theatre and enjoy performances of the city's professional Orchestra London.

Hilton London is a favourite amongst business travelers, as London is halfway between Toronto and Detroit. It is also popular with families visiting the many regional attractions including the nearby Great Lakes and the world famous Stratford Shakespearean Festival.

Photos by Mike Grandmaison

Photo by Mike Grandmaison

GM Diesel Division

Diesel Division, General Motors of Canada Limited, is London's largest manufacturing industry producing state-of-the-art freight and passenger locomotives and light armoured vehicles for the international military market. The East London plant and its 2,700 employees play a major role in the city's economy, offering jobs and training in the high-tech manufacturing sector and contracts to more than 400 supplier companies across the country.

Diesel Division, which in 2000 marked its 50th anniversary, produces an average of 350 locomotives a year for railways in Canada, the United States and 60 other countries. Its main products are 4,000 to 6,000 horsepower diesel-electric locomotives that employ modern AC traction technology and computerized control systems for maximum operational efficiency. Defence Operations has produced more than 3,500 high-speed and easily transportable light armoured vehicles, which play a major role in defence and peacekeeping duties around the world.

shopping malls sprang up where only a short time before cows had grazed. Roads widened, traffic thickened. Tall buildings began to appear downtown. By my early 20s I bucked the trend, moving into central London, drawn by the elegant Victorian architecture and shady streets.

I was married at a century-old church, where my father-in-law had been minister for many years. My sons were christened a year and three years later in the same light-filled space. With my own children, I rediscovered the city from a child's eye perspective—the neighborhood parks, the riverside bicycle path, the baseball diamonds and hockey arenas, the Children's Museum and International Children's Festival, the schools.

London is much more sophisticated and culturally diverse than it was when I was growing up. It has rich cultural offerings, a wide array of summer festivals and far more shops. The Latin Quarter was once the city's only "fine dining" spot, but now there are dozens of excellent restaurants. It remains very much a university and college town and has developed a reputation as one of Canada's premier health care and research centres. The business community, always broad-based and dynamic, has matured. The economy shows remarkable resilience and great promise.

In the first decade of the millennium, London has reached a significant point in its history. In recent years, several older firms have changed hands or moved operations. Yet the city continues to offer an attractive lifestyle and a well-educated and increasingly diverse workforce. New companies, often representing today's knowledge-based economy, are expanding and selling their products internationally. The hospitals are being reconfigured for efficiency and increased research capability, and the university is expanding. The long-neglected downtown is undergoing renewal.

I sense that London is reinventing itself. Like me, the city looks back with fondness to a comfortable past. But it also looks forward to a dynamic future, still just out of sight around the next bend. ▮

Photo by Mike Grandmaison

Accuride Canada Inc.

Accuride Canada has a long history as a leading London company that, today, is the largest commercial truck wheel plant in the world. The Firestone Boulevard plant employs more than 800, producing about 5.5 million heavy and light truck wheels and rims annually for the North American market.

Accuride Canada takes pride in its innovative approach to product development and quality control, maintaining its leadership in truck wheel production and expanding its markets. The company offers challenging, high-skilled jobs and its people participate actively in community activities, making Accuride both an economic engine for London and a respected corporate citizen.

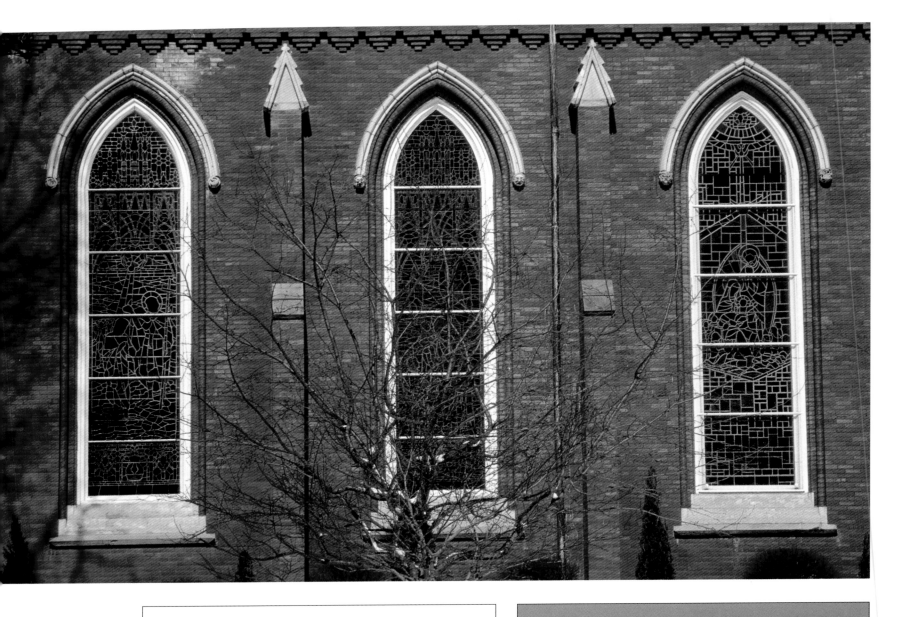

Photo by Mike Grandmaison

St. Joseph's Health Care London

St. Joseph's Health Care London has a long and distinguished history of serving the health needs of the London community, Southwestern Ontario and the veterans of Canada. As an integral part of London's hospital renewal program, St. Joseph's Hospital, Parkwood Hospital, the London/St. Thomas Psychiatric Hospital and the Mount Hope Centre for Long Term Care are joining together and taking a lead role in the next era of health care.

St. Joseph's is growing and changing to serve generations to come, just as they have met the needs of the community for many generations in the past. As a major treatment, teaching, research and care centre, St. Joseph's Health Care and its more than 4,000 staff take pride in a legacy of excellence and a shared vision for the future: "To be a respected source of excellent health service guided by the people we serve . . . provided by people who care."

Photo by Mike Grandmaison

Jones Packaging Inc.

Jones Packaging, a family-owned business with a legacy of more than a century in London, is a leading provider of innovative packaging solutions for pharmaceutical, consumer product and health-care clients across Canada, the United States and Europe. Based in a new, $15-million facility in London with a major subsidiary operation in Guelph, Ontario, Jones Packaging is recognized for its quality assurance management and use of state-of-the-art equipment and systems to meet the total packaging design and production needs of its clients.

With business roots dating back to 1882, the current company was founded by Henry J. Jones in 1920 and is today owned by Ron Harris and Christine Jones Harris, a fourth-generation family member. The company has grounded its long history in the city, and the packaging industry, with a strong commitment to its employees and a focused approach to serving its client base. One of London's landmark companies, Jones Packaging takes pride in its skilled team and their ability to succeed in the highly competitive North American, and indeed global, marketplace.

CHAPTER

TWO

Ghost Walk

The old Courthouse, built between 1827 and 1829, is supposed to be modeled on Malahide Castle, the ancestral home of Colonel Thomas Talbot, the irascible autocrat who was responsible for settling much of the area. Photo by Mike Grandmaison.

T he sun has slipped from view beyond the west bank of the River Thames. We stand at the forks of the river, where the north and south branches meet. The river path, crowded with bicyclists, rollerbladers and walkers during the day, is empty. Lights glitter in the city behind us, but here darkness spreads its pall. It is the perfect spot to begin our "Ghost Walk"—a journey into London's past.

It was this spot that John Graves Simcoe visited on a cold, damp day in March 1793. Simcoe was a military hero who served with distinction during the American War of Independence. Ten years later, he returned to North America as Lieutenant-Governor of Upper Canada. Simcoe was much taken by the site at the forks, and chose it as the future capital of Upper Canada. He set his soldiers to work building a road from Burlington Bay to the Thames River, to be called Dundas Street.

Although the site made sense to a military man—the position was easily defended—politics intervened. The capital eventually moved from Niagara to muddy York. The site at the forks of the Thames remained pristine forest until 1826, when it was chosen as the seat of government for the rapidly expanding frontier called London District.

Turn now to look up at the grim face of the jail house and beyond it, the turrets of the old Courthouse, built between 1827 and 1829. The Courthouse is supposed to be modeled on Malahide Castle, ancestral home of Colonel Thomas Talbot, the irascible autocrat who was responsible for settling much of the area. When settlers came to his handsome home at Port Talbot to ask for a grant of land, Talbot interviewed them through a small shuttered window. If he thought the supplicant was a drifter, a speculator, or worst of all, an American, Talbot slammed the window shut in his face.

Among the many dramatic events that took place in the London Courthouse was the trial of the six men accused of murdering the "Black Donnellys." A simmering feud between the Catholic Irish Donnellys and their Protestant Irish neighbors in Lucan, a village north of London, boiled over on the night of February 4, 1880. Five members of the family were murdered by a band of vigilantes. Despite eyewitness evidence, the highly publicized trial resulted in a "hung jury." At a second trial, the six men were acquitted.

The jail too has seen some bloody doings. London's first ever public hanging was held on August 19, 1830. Cornelius Burleigh, a convicted murderer, protested his innocence until hours before the execution. His "confession" was quickly printed and hawked through the crowd of 3,000 gathered to witness the solemn event. At the first attempt to carry out the sentence, the rope broke and Burleigh fell to the ground, dazed but very much alive. A second rope was fetched and the job was finished. His body was given up for dissection by medical students. A skull believed to be Burleigh's is still preserved at Eldon House.

As we walk past the tall wrought iron gates of the jailhouse, remember poor Phoebe Campbell, London's only female hanging victim, who was dispatched in 1872 to the somber sound of the tolling of the great bell in St. Paul's Cathedral.

At the top of the hill, stop for a moment and take a final look back at the river. The patch of vivid green just west of the river is Labatt Park, lit for a baseball game. The park was first built in 1876 and is reputed to be the oldest ballpark in continuous use in Canada. It was here in 1877 that the London Tecumsehs, the city's first professional ball team, won their league championship. Their victory was due in large part to pitcher Fred Goldsmith, who is believed to have invented the curveball and first practiced its black magic on the Tecumseh's hapless opponents.

Now we turn north and soon come to a row of elegant Georgianstyle brick buildings. Once known as "Banker's Row," this was London's first financial district. Until recently, the buildings served as head office for the Labatt Brewing Company, which was born in London in 1847.

Photo by Mike Grandmaison

Three generations of Labatts led the company and were prominent citizens of the city. In August, 1934, John Labatt, president of the brewery, was kidnapped by a sinister figure who signed himself "Three-Fingered Abe." Labatt was held at a cottage in Muskoka for three days before being released in Toronto. The episode is still shrouded in mystery, but some believe that the crime was linked to Prohibition-era smuggling across the Detroit River.

Turn in at the neat white gate on your left and you are in grounds of Eldon House, first built by John Harris, treasurer of the London District, in 1834. During the alarms of the Rebellion of 1837, the redoubtable Mrs. Amelia Harris and her children spent one Sunday church service making bullets for the militia. When the Rebellion was quashed, London became a British garrison town and Eldon House, with its bevy of five attractive daughters, became the centre of the town's social life. Listen carefully and you will surely hear echoes of laughter and music, as the Harrises entertain London's elite.

At one of the glittering parties, a Harris daughter watched the incoming guests eagerly, looking for her handsome British beau in his dashing dress uniform. At one point, she glanced out a window and there he was, looking in at her longingly. But to her great disappointment, he never appeared at the party. The next day, his dead body was found on the riverbank, where his horse had thrown him. His pocket watch, stopped by the impact, showed the exact time the young woman had seen him through the window.

Come, the music is fading. Let us continue our journey into the past. We turn east now and walk to Richmond Street, the city's main north-south thoroughfare. Don't let the modern façade of the Grand Theatre fool you. The theatre was first built in 1901 by Ambrose Small, one of the best-known theatrical figures in Canada. Watch the shadows carefully and you may catch a glimpse of Small himself. He disappeared under mysterious circumstances in December 1919, just after selling his chain of theaters for $1.75 million. He was a hard and irascible man, and many assumed he had been murdered. But, despite an international investigation, a body was never found. Actors alone in the building late at night have reported mysterious sights and sounds.

Out in the silken night air again, we move east past the Gothic grandeur of St. Paul's Cathedral, where once preached one of London's most colorful characters. Born near Warsaw, Poland, Isaac Hellmuth, the son of a rabbi, converted to Christianity and studied theology in England. Brought to the Diocese of Huron by Bishop Cronyn, Hellmuth was charged with establishing a theological college. Hellmuth did more: he also set up several secondary schools and founded the University of Western Ontario in 1878. He also made a start on a grand new cathedral for London, but had only completed the Chapter House by the time he resigned in 1883. The stone Chapter House has since been demolished.

The darkness deepens as we move into Victoria Park. From its earliest days London was known as "The Forest City" because it was a small clearing carved out of the brooding landscape of thick forest. By the 1870s, most of the original trees had been cleared and Londoners

were developing a new appreciation for shade. The new park was laid out and thickly planted with young trees. Trees were also planted on boulevards throughout London—a practice that continues today and gave new meaning to the name "The Forest City."

It was in Victoria Park that Cy Warman, an American railway worker and part-time poet, was inspired by his beloved Myrtle Marie Jones, a local high school student, to write the words to "Sweet

The site at the forks of the Thames remained a pristine forest until 1826, when it was chosen as the seat of government for the rapidly expanding frontier called London District, and settlers began making their homes here. Photo by Mike Grandmaison.

Marie." The words, set to music by Raymond Moore, became a popular song, and later a popular chocolate bar. Warman married his sweet Marie and they lived for many years in a large house in North London. If you catch a glimpse of the shades of two Victorian lovers strolling in the park, don't be afraid—they are happy souls.

A block south of the Park we pass the hallowed walls of the London Club. This opulent structure was built in 1881 as a haven for financiers, businessmen and politicians and remained a mens-only club for more than 100 years. It's likely that the Cuban cigars puffed by prosperous members of the club in the late nineteenth century were made in London: cigar manufacturing was a major local industry during the '80s and '90s. Among the wealthiest men who gathered at

(above) Among the many dramatic events that took place in the London Courthouse was the trial of six men accused of murdering the "Black Donnellys" when a simmering feud between the Catholic Irish Donnellys and their Protestant Irish neighbors north of London supposedly boiled over on the night of February 4, 1880. However, the six men were eventually acquitted of the crime. Photo by Mike Grandmaison.

(below) London became genteel as the Victorian Era progressed, with more settlers establishing neighborhoods and businesses in the area. Photo by Mike Grandmaison.

the club were London's oil barons. Oil was discovered in southwestern Ontario in the 1860s and by the '70s "oil fever" was rampant. Fortunes were made, and sometimes lost, in days.

We now walk south and east, into the heart of London's current downtown. At the corner of Clarence and Dundas Streets, the elaborate façade of the former "Mechanic's Institute" is preserved on the second and third floors. The building, constructed in 1877, was a precursor of the public library. Later it became a music hall, and the site of one of London's most notorious killings.

The terrible deed occurred on April 1, 1898. The touring Wesley Stock Company was performing a play called "The Candidate," billed as a satire on Canadian politics. Just before the play was about to start, the curtain rose to reveal a man holding a smoking revolver, with a body stretched at his feet. The man with the gun was William Emerson, an American actor, and the corpse was James Tuttle, manager of the company. At first, the audience took it all as an elaborate April Fool's joke. When they realized it wasn't, confusion reigned. In the ensuing trial, it became clear that Tuttle and Emerson had been arguing about overdue wages. The gun Emerson fired was a stage property, but loaded with live ammunition. Londoners sided with the actor and sympathized with his lovely actress

wife. The verdict was "not guilty." It would be no wonder if James Tuttle still haunted the site of his murder, seeking justice .

As we stroll down Dundas Street back toward the river, we are entering the haunts of Dr. Neill Cream, an infamous murderer who lived and practiced as a doctor in London for several years. Cream narrowly avoided being charged with murder after one of his patients, a young chambermaid, was discovered dead in an alley near his office, a bottle of chloroform lying beside her. Cream continued his career of crime in Chicago, where he served a jail sentence, and eventually returned to London, England. Some have proposed him as the true identity of the infamous Jack the Ripper, although the connection has never been proved. He was hanged on November 15, 1892.

And now we approach the river again. The water slips silently under the bridge, but its gentleness is deceptive. London's worst disaster took place on the river on a bright day in May 1881.

During the late 1870s, London's City Council bought land down river from the city to build a municipal waterworks. The new land became a popular picnic spot, most easily reached by steamer from the forks of the Thames. On May 24, 1881, a public holiday to honor the Queen's birthday, hundreds of Londoners, laden with well-filled picnic

baskets, boarded steamers for Waterworks Park. Late that afternoon an overcrowded steamer capsized during a return journey. Weighed down by their heavy clothes or crushed when the ship's boiler came loose, at least 181 people were killed, most of them women and children.

The river struck again, in a different way, two years later. During a freak summer storm in 1883, the Thames River burst its banks and roared through West London, destroying hundreds of homes and killing 18. Other floods followed, including a devastating one in 1938. Eventually a dam was built north of the city.

It is time to return to the 21st century. But don't let this Ghost Walk mislead you. London's colorful inhabitants were not all miscreants. The cast of thousands includes canny businessmen, colorful eccentrics, generous philanthropists, courageous military figures, dashing athletes, silver-tongued politicians, gentle healers and gifted artists and writers. It's a story of effort and achievement, a triumph of innovation and energy.

It is, of course, far easier to travel back in time, than forward. But based on what we have learned of London's past, the future will be anything but dull. ▮

The beautiful Thames has a deceptive gentleness. Twice the river has been the site of disaster, first in 1881 when at least 181 people were killed when a steamer capsized on a return journey from Waterworks Park, and again in 1883 when a summer storm swelled the river until it escaped its banks and roared through West London, destroying hundreds of homes and killing 18. After several other floods throughout the years, eventually a dam was built north of the city. Photo by Mike Grandmaison.

(left) Eldon House was built by John Harris, treasurer of the London District, in 1834, and eventually became the centre of the town's social life. Legend holds that one of the Harris daughters waited anxiously at a party for her beau, a British soldier. She caught a glimpse of him outside the window, but he never came in to join the party. The next day, his body was found on the riverbank, apparently thrown from his horse. His watch had stopped—at the exact time the young woman had claimed to see him through the window. Photos by Mike Grandmaison.

(below) London's first ever public hanging was held at the old jail, on August 19, 1830. Cornelius Burleigh had been convicted of murder, but continued to protest his innocence up to the execution hour. The story has it that on the first attempt to carry out the sentence, the rope broke and Burleigh fell to the ground. A second rope was fetched and the task was completed. The body was donated to medical students, and a skull believed to be Burleigh's is still preserved at Eldon House.

(opposite) It was in Victoria Park that Cy Warman, an American railway worker and part-time poet, was inspired by his beloved Myrtle Marie Jones, a local high school student, to write the words to "Sweet Marie." The words, set to music by Raymond Moore, became a popular song, and later a popular chocolate bar.

3

T H R E E

Making Connections

London is located in the industrial heartland of North America, within a day's drive of 150 million people, and well-connected by road, rail, and air to major business centres like Toronto, Detroit, Chicago, New York, and Montreal. London is also the rail hub for Southwestern Ontario, connecting the region to the rest of Canada and to the U.S. Photo by Mike Grandmaison.

L ondoners often boast about living in "the most connected city" in Canada.
Certainly, London is located in the industrial heartland of North America, within a day's drive
of 150 million people. The city is well connected by road, rail and air to major business centres
like Toronto, Detroit, Chicago, New York, and Montreal.

London boasts an advanced telecommunications infrastructure, truly the super-highway of the new millennium. Photo by Mike Grandmaison.

But when Londoners talk about connectedness, they are also talking about an advanced telecommunications infrastructure, truly the superhighway of the new millennium. In the 21st century, the movement of electronic bits and bytes is just as important as the movement of people and goods—and London is well positioned to do both.

Draw a line between Toronto and Detroit, and you'll find London at the midpoint. The city is located on two major highways: 401, which connects Montreal to Windsor/Detroit; and 402, which runs from London to Sarnia/Port Huron, Michigan. Both highways provide rapid and easy access to U.S. markets. It is estimated that $129 billion of trade flows across the border between Ontario and Michigan each year. Some 7,700 trucks drive by London every day on the Highway 401, and that number is expected to increase dramatically.

Plans are currently being developed to create a "NAFTA superhighway," a seamless, high quality road link connecting the three partners of the North America Free Trade Agreement. The northern portion of the NAFTA superhighway will flow along either the 401 or the 402 or both, ensuring that London-based businesses profit from new opportunities for north-south trade.

London is also the rail hub for Southwestern Ontario, connecting the region to the rest of Canada and to the U.S.. London's VIA Station is the fourth busiest rail terminal in Canada for passenger travel, with more than 180,000 passengers between January and June 1999. Business connections to and from Toronto are excellent, with trains from early morning to early evening. CN has plans to build a new terminal in the city, an intermodal facility that will provide easy connections with air and bus service. London also has excellent rail freight service.

For a few days in June, the skies of London roar and the city becomes a mecca for aviation enthusiasts. Airshow London and Balloon Festival, one of Canada's premier air shows, attracts 50,000 fans each year. The show is held at the London International Airport, a facility located just 11 kilometres east of the city core.

Five scheduled air carriers operate through London International Airport: Air Ontario, Ontario Regional Airlines, USAirways Express, London Air and Northwest AirLink. World of Vacations operates charter flight services and Emery Worldwide, Air Canada Cargo and Dynamex Courier provide air cargo services. In total, the 24-hour facility handles 72 flights daily and is the tenth busiest in Canada.

The airport is run by the Greater London International Airport Authority, a non-profit, community-based corporation. The Authority is working to increase the number of Londoners who begin their journeys in London (rather than driving to Toronto or Detroit) and to increase air cargo volume. It has plans to expand and upgrade the terminal building, add additional air services and attract related commercial developments.

The airport's two main tenants are Air Ontario and Diamond Aircraft Canada Corp., a manufacturer renowned for its single engine, two-seater flight trainer. Air Ontario, a subsidiary of Air Canada, carries more than one million passengers annually to 23 destinations throughout central Canada and the northeastern U.S.

Transportation links are essential for moving goods to markets across North America. But the highways of the electronic economy are high speed fiber optic cables, able to transmit huge amounts of information anywhere in the world, instantly. London's fully-digital, self-healing fiber optics telecommunications infrastructure provides a strong base for knowledge-based industries and services. The system offers high speed, high quality, reliable service. Through the use of advanced remote access technologies, the fiber optics network now reaches 85 per cent of London customers.

This powerful infrastructure, coupled with an ethnically diverse population and the excellent training programs developed by Fanshawe College, has generated explosive growth in the call centre industry. There are 35 call centres in London, including Oracle, The Assistance Group, Alliance, London Free Press, Union Gas and Canada Trust. In all the industry employs 3,000 to 3,500 people directly and many more in related businesses. Through the Call Centre Advisory Board, local call centre managers get together to share ideas and solve problems cooperatively.

Canada Trust operates a national call center in London in support of its EasyLine telephone banking service, EasyWeb internet service and direct marketing operations. Between London and the back-up centre in St. John, New Brunswick, Canada Trust operators handle 35 million calls a year. Canada Trust also offers service in Cantonese and Mandarin from its London location. Locating the service in a city the size of London allowed Canada Trust to build a model call centre in its own building with at-the-door parking.

Bell Canada operates a regional headquarters in London, employing more than 1,300 people. It is Bell's advanced technology that puts a wide range of innovative voice and data services at the fingertips of

Some 7,700 trucks drive by London every day on the Highway 401, and that number is expected to increase dramatically with the establishment of the "NAFTA superhighway," a seamless, high-quality road link connecting the three partners of the North America Free Trade Agreement. The NAFTA superhighway will flow along either the 401 or 402. Photos by Mike Grandmaison.

(above) London's fully digital, self-healing fiber optics telecommunications infrastructure provides a strong foundation for knowledge-based industries and services. Bell Canada operates a regional headquarters in London, employing more than 1,300 people and putting a wide range of innovative voice and data services at the fingertips of Londoners. Photo by Mike Grandmaison.

(below) London is located at the midpoint between Toronto and Detroit, served by two major highways: 401, which connects Montreal to Windsor/Detroit; and 402, which runs from London to Sarnia/Port Huron, Michigan. Photo by Mike Grandmaison.

Londoners. In fact, a portion of the city was chosen as a trial market for TotalVision, which provides access to 100 TV channels and FM radio stations, digital video, CD quality audio programming and high speed Internet connections. London was chosen because of the city's many well-educated, high-income consumers with a demonstrated interest in new technologies. The city has also been used to test market other new products, including VISTA 350, a phone that provides access to interactive banking, entertainment and shopping services. Community Express, Bell's community multimedia centre, provides Internet based services for not-for-profit community organizations.

London Hydro, the city's electricity utility, is also contributing to London's reputation as "the most connected city." In April 1999, Hydro launched an innovative Internet access service, Londonconnect, based on a fiber optic network strung over existing power lines. The service offers wide bandwidth connection, giving London businesses high-speed voice, data and video exchange at a reasonable cost. London Hydro is one of very few municipal utilities that have entered the telecommunications business, and leads the way in progress on its infrastructure.

Recognizing the enormous potential of e-commerce, local and regional organizations are working together to expand and strengthen London's connectivity. An example is LargeNet, a non profit organization focused on city-wide and regional networking. The objective of LargeNet is to connect London organizations to one another and provide high-speed access to the Internet. The network now includes London hospitals, the university, Fanshawe College, the public library system and the City of London and connects to the neighboring communities of Woodstock and St. Thomas. Through a partnership with Bell Canada and LargeNet, even London students have high speed access to the Internet through their schools. ◄

London International Airport is located just 11 kilometres east of the city core. Five scheduled air carriers operate through the facility—Air Ontario, Ontario Regional Airlines, USAirways Express, London Air, and Northwest AirLink. Additionally, World of Vacations operates charter flight services, and Emery Worldwide, Air Canada Cargo, and Dyanmex Courier provide air cargo services. In total, the 24-hour facility handles seventy-two flights daily and is the tenth busiest in Canada. Photos by Mike Grandmaison.

F O U R

Branding London

Given London's location in the midst of some of the richest agricultural land in Canada, it's not surprising that food processing is an important manufacturing sector. Kellogg Canada, for example, has made cereal in London since early in the century. Some 700,000 cartons of cereal are produced each day, and 25 per cent of the total volume is exported. Photo by Mike Grandmaison.

I t was an unusual and compelling sight: the arrival in June 1999 of eight new 350,000 litre fermenting tanks destined for Labatt Breweries London brewery.

Some Londoners were frustrated by the traffic hold-ups caused by the trucks carrying the huge vats as they rumbled their way north from Highway 401 to their eventual home in downtown London. But most were intrigued and heartened. After all, the event was a concrete expression of a $50-million expansion at Labatt's London operation. The expansion includes an additional 30,000 square feet of production space, a new bottling line capable of processing 900 bottles per minute, the fermenting tanks and several other major pieces of equipment.

London builder Ellis Don constructed the SkyDome, home of the Toronto Blue Jays baseball team, and many other high-profile projects around the world. Founded in 1956, Ellis Don now has operations in ten American states and has completed projects in ten different countries. Photo by Mike Grandmaison.

The heart of Labatt's export business in Ontario, the London plant was being expanded to meet the demand for Labatt brands in the U.S. Labatt's Blue, in particular, has become very successful, even outselling domestic beers in some U.S. markets. In 1998 Labatt exports to the U.S. increased by almost 20 per cent, and the company expects the growth to continue.

Labatt's has a long history in London. The firm was founded as a pioneer brewery in the 1840s and grew rapidly, fed by demand created by the British garrison stationed in the city. By the 1880s, the company was producing 322,000 barrels a year, six times its capacity at the outset. After World War II Labatt's went public and opened new plants across Canada. Today the company is truly international, with interests in Europe, Mexico, the Caribbean and South America. Yet the London operation is still important.

Labatt's is one of many manufacturing companies that take advantage of London's strong workforce and excellent location to make products sold across Canada, throughout North America and around the world. Each time a Labatt Blue is sold in western New York state, it carries the London "brand" with it. In fact, the company introduced a special label bearing the legend "proudly brewed in London" during 1999.

It's not just beer bottles that carry the London "brand" to the world. It goes forth on everything from automobiles and breakfast cereal, to wheel rims and faucets. Although London is sometimes thought of as a "white collar" city, manufacturing is a major driver of the economy, employing 138,000 people and creating 7,000 new jobs in 1999.

Among its head offices, London includes the Canadian headquarters for 3M, a powerful multinational company with operations in 60 countries and an enviable reputation for innovation. Products like Scotch tape and Post-it notes are literally household names, but the company also produces overhead projectors, earthquake-proof window coverings, fibre optics, surgical drape, fabric protector, cleaning pads, Thinsulate insulation and much more.

3M Canada was established in London in 1952, partly because the city provided easy access to automotive customers for industrial abrasive products. The Canadian head office is responsible for sales of almost $900 million annually and employs more than 2,000 people in London and in plants in Ontario, Quebec and Manitoba. Up to 75 per cent of what is produced in Canada is exported to the U.S. and to other 3M subsidiaries in 30 countries.

Another company that carries London's brand to the world is GM Diesel, which celebrates its 50th anniversary in 2000. Eighty per cent of the freight and passenger locomotives currently at work in Canada were born in London. Today GM employs 2,700 Londoners and sells locomotives in 60 countries around the world. Major locomotive customers include the English Welsh & Scottish Railway, the Burlington Northern and Santa Fe Railway and the Union Pacific. GM Diesel is also a large supplier of locomotives to Algeria, Tunisia and India. In late 1999 the company finalized a $2-billion deal to supply 1,000 new locomotives to Union Pacific.

The London operation has also developed a strong defence component. In 1977 the company was approached by the Canadian government, which was in the market for a new defence vehicle. They were looking at a Swiss-made design and asked if the company would be interested in building it. The skills required were very similar to those for building locomotives and other diesel powered vehicles, so GM Diesel agreed.

Twenty years later, the London plant has become a centre of world excellence in the design and manufacture of Light Armoured Vehicles (LAVs). The defence division has built more than 3,000 vehicles for clients that include the Canadian Armed Forces, the United States Marine Corps and National guard, the Australian Army and Saudi Arabia. GM Diesel vehicles have served in military and peacekeeping operations around the world, including Cyprus, Panama, Somalia and Bosnia. They saw action in the hands of the United States Marine Corps in Operation Desert Storm. In late 1999 the Canadian Armed Forces placed a $247-million order for armored personnel carriers.

Automotive manufacturing is a strong component of the local economy, a byproduct of London's location close to the U.S. border and the impact of the auto pact. The Ford plant just to the south and the CAMI plant to the east of the city each employ hundreds of Londoners. CAMI, a joint venture between General Motors of Canada and Suzuki Motor Corporation, was opened in 1989 in Ingersoll, Ontario. The plant, which employs 2,400, produces small sport utility vehicles and economy passenger cars. The Ford plant in St. Thomas, which builds Ford Crown Victoria and Mercury Grand Marquis models, has won several quality awards, including the J.D. Power Plant Quality Award for top Ford plant in North America in 1998.

Other automotive plants in the London area include Accuride Canada, which manufactures wheels and rims for the truck, trailer and bus industries and Freightliner, which produces heavy-duty trucks in its St. Thomas plant. Siemens Electric Limited manufactures some 11 million electric motors a year for installation in Chrysler, Ford, BMW, Volkswagen, Volvo, Audi and GM vehicles. Siemens is the first company in the world to mass-produce brushless electric motors for the automotive industry. These motors last longer, run quieter and interface better with the engine management system of your vehicle.

Given London's location in the midst of some of the richest agricultural land in Canada, it's not surprising that food processing is an important manufacturing sector. Kellogg Canada, for example, has made cereal in London since early in the century.

Labatt Breweries has recently expanded its London operation, adding $50 million worth of facilities and equipment to meet the growing demand for Labatt brands in the United States. In addition to its economic contributions to the city's economy, the company sponsored the construction of Labatt Park. Photo courtesy Tourism London.

The plant began as the Canada Corn Company, a manufacturing facility with the rights to produce Toasted Corn Flakes for Canadian distribution, but was bought by W.K. Kellogg in 1924. In 1986 the plant underwent a $223-million expansion, making it one of the most technologically advanced cereal manufacturing facilities in the world. Computer-automated machinery performs all steps of production and an advanced monorail system carries in-process food through the plant. Some 700,000 cartons of cereal are produced each day, and 25 per cent of the total volume is exported.

Another large food producer got its start in Strathroy, a small town just outside London that enjoys the honor of being Canada's turkey capital. It was the birthplace of Cuddy International Corporation, now headquartered in London. Starting with a 100-acre farm, company founder Mac Cuddy developed innovative ways to improve productivity of turkey poults and eggs, including artificial insemination and the use of artificial light to alter laying patterns. The company grew rapidly, eventually expanding into turkey processing and feed. Today it has operations in the U.S. and Europe, and produces 120 different chicken and turkey products.

Other food-related manufacturers in London include Casco, which produces liquid sugar products; McCormick & Company, which processes herbs, spices and other food flavorings; and Masterfeeds, a national animal feed company.

When the skies darken and rain threatens during a Toronto Blue Jays home game, spectators are treated to an extra show, thanks to another leading London company. To the accompaniment of audible oohs and aahs, the 50,000-seat stadium's retractable roof gradually moves into place. London builder Ellis Don built the SkyDome and many other high-profile projects around the world. Founded in 1956, Ellis Don now has operations in ten American states and has completed projects in ten different countries. One of its most exciting recent projects was the new span of the Blue Water Bridge, which joins Sarnia, Ontario, with Port Huron, Michigan.

London also supports a cluster of other companies in the building industry, including Kaiser Aluminum, Delta Faucet and EMCO Limited. EMCO started life as The Empire Manufacturing Company, a foundry in downtown London. Today, the company, which is owned by U.S.-based Masco Corporation, distributes and manufactures products for the construction industry, including pipes and valves for water works and roof shingles. Sales in 1998 were $1.24 billion. Delta Faucet Canada, also owned by Masco, started in Wallaceburg, an hour's drive west of London, almost 100 years ago. With annual sales of more than $10 million, Delta Canada employs close to 500 people. The London plant of Wolverine Tube, an

international company with plants across North America, produces seamless copper and copper alloy tubes in a wide variety of sizes for plumbing and industrial use.

London's superb location, good road connections and skilled work force mean that manufacturing will continue to play an important role in the city's growth. But senior managers consistently cite another factor in explaining their companies' success in London: the city's laid-back lifestyle encourages workers and managers to settle and remain in the city. At Kellogg, for example, 70 per cent of the employees have worked at the plant for more than 10 years. A good environment for business and a great place to live—both essential elements in the London brand. ◗

(above left) 3M Canada was established in London in 1952. Today, the Canadian head office is responsible for sales of almost $900 million annually and employs more than 2,000 people in London and in plants in Ontario, Quebec, and Manitoba. The company produces such well-known products as Scotch tape and Post-it notes, as well as items including overhead projectors, surgical drape, cleaning pads, and much more. Photo by Mike Grandmaison.

(below) The Ford assembly plant in St. Thomas is among London's outstanding auto manufacturing ventures that employ thousands in the area and produce products for use throughout the world by corporations, governmental agencies, and individuals. Photo courtesy of Victor Aziz.

(opposite) One London Place, a dominant skyscraper in the London skyline, is a visual representation of the London economy and its ever-upward track toward success. Photo by Mike Grandmaison.

FIVE

Leaders in the
Knowledge Economy

London is home to more than five hundred high-tech firms in a wide range of
industries, including several well-established companies and many promising
start-ups. A new biotechnology incubator, scheduled to open in 2001, will
provide additional impetus for growth. Photo by Mike Grandmaison.

W hen it comes to "sexy" technology, London's Virtual Environment Technology Centre is a winner. The centre is part of the Integrated Manufacturing Technologies Institute (IMTI), a National Research Council facility located on the University of Western Ontario (UWO) Research park. VETC uses virtual reality computer software to help manufacturers design prototypes faster and more accurately. Virtual reality allows manufacturers to see and "feel" products and processes. Considered the world's most advanced virtual reality facility when it opened in fall 1999, the center allows product designers and engineers to view their concept from every angle, even from inside out. The "Immersive Theatre" seats up to 25 people for group presentations in the virtual reality mode. Immersive workrooms and design rooms allow smaller groups to use the facility. Although designed primarily for use in manufacturing, this advanced technology also has applications in medicine, architecture, urban planning and other fields.

The Integrated Manufacturing Technologies Institute (IMTI), which employs about 100 people, also houses Canada's largest and most advanced industrial laser laboratory, used for work in the field of free form fabrication. The facility is designed to bridge the gap between basic science research and industrial problem-solving, and to provide Canadian industry with a competitive advantage in innovative design and production.

The IMTI is a critical component of London's rapidly growing high-tech sector. The city is home to more than 500 high tech firms in a wide range of industries, including several well-established companies and many promising start-ups. The new biotechnology incubator, scheduled to open in 2001, will provide additional impetus for growth.

Trudell Medical Group is one of London's oldest and best-established high tech companies. The company produces aerosol delivery devices and asthma management products, including a line of aerosol delivery devices for horses, and sells its products in 70 countries worldwide. The company also has divisions that manufacture lithotripters (devices that fragment urinary system stones using shock waves), distribute specialized hospital equipment and supply home oxygen.

Trojan Technologies Inc., another leading representative of London's high-tech sector, designs and manufactures ultraviolet light applications for disinfection of drinking water and treatment of municipal wastewater. Trojan's technology, considered more environmentally friendly than chemical disinfection, is now in use in thousands of municipal installations around the world.

And that's just the tip of London's high-tech iceberg. Among many other exciting enterprises:

- Diamond Aircraft manufactures the Katana, a series of light planes for training and private owner use.
- Sparton Electronics provides electronic contract design and manufacturing services, including high quality printed circuit board design and manufacturing, prototyping and testing.
- KGK Synergize Inc. develops nutraceuticals and functional foods with anti-cancer and cholesterol-lowering potential, and provides contract research services for evaluation of natural and synthetic products.
- Microtronix is a group of companies producing telephone testing equipment, communication networking products and software solutions for enterprise systems.
- Coral Technologies is a leading system integrator.
- Sonometrics Corporation manufactures sophisticated sonic measurement and guidance devices for medical treatment and research.
- Phoenix Interactive Design Inc. develops customer interfaces for banking machines.

- Life Imaging Systems, a spin-off from research conducted at London's hospitals and research institutes, designs and manufactures 3D ultrasound imaging products.
- Purifics Environmental Technologies Inc. builds photocatalytic water treatment equipment.
- Viron Therapeutics is developing protein therapies for the treatment of asthma, arthritis and transplant rejection.
- Diabetogen is focused on discovering and developing new chemical and biological products for the prevention and treatment of Type 1 diabetes.
- Multi Magnetic, another spin-off from London's research community, develops MRI technology for various medical applications.
- BLES Biochemical develops naturally occurring surfactants for neonatal care.
- Thinkspace develops geographical information systems software for use in business, education and government. It recently licensed an education package with the Ontario Ministry of Education for use in 800 schools.
- Fra-lex Therapeutics develops bioelectromagnetic therapies.

The London High Technology Association provides an informal forum for these companies to exchange ideas and solve problems. Through its volunteer board, the Association also promotes high technology, educates its members and represents the high tech community in the London region.

(opposite) Diamond Aircraft manufactures the Katana, a series of light planes for training and private-owner use. Photo by Mike Grandmaison.

(above) Trudell Medical Group is one of London's oldest and best-established high-tech companies. The company produces aerosol delivery devices and asthma management products, and sells its products in seventy countries worldwide. Photo by Mike Grandmaison.

(top) Trojan Technologies Inc. designs and manufactures ultraviolet light applications for disinfection of drinking water and treatment of municipal waste-water. Trojan's treatment methods are considered more environmentally friendly than chemical disinfection. Photo by Mike Grandmaison.

(below) Purifics Environmental Technologies Inc. builds photocatalytic water treatment equipment. Photo courtesy of Purifics.

Like the IMTI, The University of Western Ontario is an important resource for companies with a science or technology base. The Office of Industry Liaison provides an entry point to all technology development and research activities at UWO, including the Applied Electrostatics Research Centre, the Boundary Layer Wind Tunnel, the Centre for Interdisciplinary Studies in Chemical Physics, the Chemical Reactor Engineering Centre, the Geotechnical Research Centre, Interface Science Western, the Power Engineering Analysis and Research Laboratory, the Research Centre in Tribology and Surface Science Western.

London's rich agricultural hinterland is also becoming part of the high-tech revolution, through the introduction of "molecular farming." Molecular farming is the science of growing vaccines and other beneficial products in plants and animals, through genetic modification. Scientists at the Siebens-Drake Research Institute in London have begun producing Interleukin-10 (a protein used to fight Crohn's disease) in tobacco plants. Plantigen, a start-up company located at the London Health Sciences Centre, is developing and testing plants that produce therapeutic proteins for the prevention of autoimmune diseases like diabetes and transplant rejection. London was the site for a major international conference on molecular farming in the fall of 1999.

Molecular farming is just one aspect of biotechnology, an industry that has grown from a worldwide capitalization of $50 million in 1985 to $120 billion by 1998. London, with its world-class university and large medical community, has identified biotech as a focus for economic development activities. In late 1999, City Council voted to invest $5 million in the construction of a biotechnology incubator. The Province of Ontario also provided funding. The incubator, currently under construction at the UWO Research Park, will provide start-up biotech ventures with office and lab space, reception and meeting rooms, IT infrastructure, management and legal expertise and other services. In this low-cost environment, these young companies will be able to grow to the point where they can stand on their own.

Traditionally a manufacturing center, London is clearly poised to make its mark in the economy of the 21st century. ❙◀

(right) The University of Western Ontario Research Park is an incubator for more than twenty innovative organizations and businesses, many of them spin-offs from university research, and is also the location of the National Research Council's Integrated Manufacturing Technology Institute. Photo by Mike Grandmaison.

(below) Educational opportunities in the field of high technology are diverse throughout London, with programs including traditional four-year universities and colleges, technical schools and training programs, and many other options. Pictured is the CDI College of Business and Technology. Photo by Mike Grandmaison.

Mind and Spirit

The London Public Library has been a valued part of city life for more than 100 years. It is headquartered in an impressive Depression-era building on Queens Avenue, and operates fourteen branches in various parts of the city, with a total circulation of more than 3.5 million. Photo by Mike Grandmaison.

During a single week in September, London is awakened from its summer somnolence by an explosion of activity. Thousands of students arrive in town to attend Fanshawe College and The University of Western Ontario. Moving trucks are a common sight. Quiet neighborhoods are suddenly filled with music and laughter. And for a day, the streets come alive with students raising money for the Canadian Cystic Fibrosis Foundation.

London offers outstanding primary and secondary education through two school boards, the Thames Valley District School Board (TVDSB) and the London District Catholic School Board (LDCSB), and a variety of private schools. Photo courtesy of Tourism London.

Shinerama, as this annual fundraiser is called, has been a tradition at Western for more than 30 years. In addition to simply canvassing passersby, students plan a variety of wacky stunts and fun activities to draw attention to the cause. In 1999 Fanshawe students also became involved. Western has raised more money for Shinerama than any other university each year for the past 14 years. By 1998, the total Western contribution had reached $1.5 million.

Shinerama is a symbol of the symbiotic relationship between London and its educational institutions. As a university town for almost 125 years and a college town since 1967, the city provides a warm welcome and a comfortable lifestyle for students, professors and researchers from around the world. Increasingly, London's educational sector is being recognized as a lynchpin in plans for economic development.

Fanshawe College, founded in 1967, was one of the first community colleges in Ontario, designed to meet the growing need for advanced training in employment skills. The college now offers more than 85 post-secondary programs and 4,000 course workshops and seminars, at campuses in London, St. Thomas, Simcoe and Woodstock. Although originally founded to serve the needs of the London area, Fanshawe is involved in projects, and welcomes students from, around the world. Fourteen thousand full-time and 40,000 part-time students take advantage of Fanshawe's learning opportunities. Enrolment has increased by almost 40 per cent between 1990 and 1998. A recent grant from the Ontario government will allow the college to expand and thus meet the growing demand.

Fanshawe's offerings are diverse, from business and health care to computer technology, electronics, environmental technology, hospitality and human services. Many Fanshawe diploma programs include a co-operative education component, requiring students to get practical experience by working in their chosen industry. In recent years, the college has developed a number of innovative "post-diploma" programs offering both college and university graduates career training in areas such as corporate communications, web system analysis and organizational learning and development.

The college sees itself as playing an important role in promoting and serving economic development in the City. Representatives from local business and industry are invited to sit on program advisory committees, which provide input into the curricula, ensuring that each program reflects the rapidly changing realities of its industry. Priding itself on flexibility and responsiveness, the college reviews most programs at least every five years. Effectively, London companies have an opportunity to ensure that graduating students have the skills they're looking for in employees.

To meet the growing need to develop human capital, the college operates a contract training service. When a local business buys a new software package or piece of manufacturing equipment, or identifies other training needs, it can turn to Fanshawe to develop a customized training program, deliverable on-site or at the college.

Among other facilities that Fanshawe offers the London community are a modern fitness centre open to members of the community, a fully licensed dining room and deli, staffed by students training in the hospitality field and several child care centres. The College's many continuing education offerings address a wide range of interests and needs, from strictly recreational to career-specific.

The contrast between the starkly modern architecture of the Fanshawe campus and the "Collegiate Gothic" of Western's seems to underline the differences in the two institutions. Yet there is increasing recognition that the two must work together to respond to the changing environment for their graduates.

Founded in 1878 by the Anglican Diocese of Huron, the university almost foundered in its early years for lack of funding. In 1908, it was put on a firm footing when it became a nondenominational university. Today, the university consists of 12 faculties, including Medicine and Dentistry, Law, Engineering and Education and three affiliated colleges and offers more than 50 different degree and diploma programs. With 26,000 students and 5,500 full-and part-time employees, Western is the city's second largest employer, and a small city in its own right. Western generates an estimated $1 billion in local economic activity on an annual basis and attracts external research grants totaling more than $85 million.

The number of students applying to and registering at Western has increased steadily for the past three years. A recent survey of Western's class of '96 graduates showed that 97.9 per cent were employed after two years, and 92.8 per cent were employed after six months. In February 2000, the university received $40.5 million from a special provincial program set up to fund educational expansion. The money is being used to build two new classroom buildings and expand in several other areas.

The university's Industry Liaison Office builds bridges between Western's outstanding researchers and the corporate world. The office helps faculty members develop collaborative projects and provides industry with easy access to Western expertise, research networks and equipment. The University of Western Ontario Research Park is an incubator for more than 20 innovative organizations and businesses, many of them spin-offs from university research, and is also the location of the National Research Council's Integrated Manfacturing Technologies Institute.

The university is currently in the process of upgrading its research facilities for the new millennium. In the plans is an Integrated Research Institute that will house several new research centres, including the National Centre for Audiology, the Centre for Integrated Product and Process Design, the Institute for Catastrophic Loss Reduction and the Centre for Electrical Energy Systems. The university's proposed Advanced Biotechnology Research Centre will bring together investigators from across the campus to undertake biotechnology, medical and bioengineering research, using the most advanced technology, instrumentation and training. Western's existing and planned research capacity represents a major asset for local industry.

The Richard Ivey School of Business, an integral part of the university, is ranked among the best business schools in the world. Ivey offers undergraduate, graduate and executive programs and generates applied research and business cases in a wide range of fields. The school also operates a permanent campus in Hong Kong, the Asian Management Institute, the Institute for Entrepreneurship, Innovation and Growth, and a low-cost business consulting service.

St. Thomas Aquinas is a Catholic school that is part of the LDCSB, which operates 50 elementary schools and six secondary schools serving more than 22,000 students. Photo by Mike Grandmaison.

Like Fanshawe, Western's campus is a resource for the people for Southwestern Ontario, providing a wide range of continuing education offerings, both on campus and via distance education, as well as recreational opportunities. The campus, itself a London landmark, is home to an excellent small theatre, large and small concert halls and two art galleries. Intercollegiate sports, especially football and basketball, are closely followed by local fans. Thanks to the presence of Western, Londoners have access to such facilities as:

- The Canadian Centre for Activity and Ageing, a research facility that also provides outreach and support programs
- The Glen Cairn Community Nursing Resource Centre, which provides wellness education and assistance for people facing challenges due to socio-economic factors
- The School of Dentistry clinic, providing low-cost dental care
- The Fowler-Kennedy Sport Medicine Clinic, a world-class facility that serves thousands of Londoners with athletic injuries
- The city also has a number of excellent private vocational schools, including Westervelt College, a London fixture for more than 100 years.

London offers outstanding primary and secondary education through two school boards, the Thames Valley District School Board (TVDSB) and the London District Catholic School Board (LDCSB), and a variety of private schools. The LDCSB consists of 50 elementary and six secondary schools serving more than 22,000 students. The TVDSB is the third largest board of education in Ontario, with 160 elementary schools, 31 secondary schools and a student population of 90,000. Both Boards offer French Immersion, programs for students with special needs, English as a Second Language instruction and adult education opportunities.

(above) *Fanshawe College was founded in 1967 as one of the first community colleges in Ontario, designed to meet the growing need for advanced training in employment skills. The college now offers more than eighty-five post-secondary programs and four thousand course workshops and seminars at campuses in London, St. Thomas, Simcoe, and Woodstock. Photo by Mike Grandmaison.*

(opposite) *The University of Western Ontario was founded in 1878 by the Anglican Diocese of Huron. Today, the university consists of twelve faculties, including Medicine and Dentistry, Law, Engineering, and Education, and three affiliated colleges, and offers more than fifty different degree and diploma programs. The University serves 26,000 students and has 5,500 full- and part-time employees, making it the city's second largest employer. Photo by Mike Grandmaison.*

The London Investment in Education Council, which was incorporated in 1993, is an innovative partnership between the corporate and education sectors, designed to maximize learning opportunities for Londoners. Among its innovative programs are:

• Bridges, a program that has developed 15 secondary school credit courses in job-specific skills for students leaving school early
• Kids Count, a community-driven program to promote better health and learning opportunities in high risk, low income neighborhoods
• Read-Write-Now, a program to develop a volunteer pool to implement literacy strategies in schools

LIEC also presents an annual learning conference that brings together educators, business people and other members of the community.

Another innovative program born in London and offered collaboratively by the private and education sectors is Global Vision. The brainchild of Terry Clifford, a former London-area MP, Global Vision is a national program that provides opportunities for secondary school and university students to discover and experience the world of international business. Global Vision offers conferences, internships and a "Junior Team Canada Trade Mission" travel experience.

London's strong educational sector ensures that the city has a well-educated workforce, excellent facilities for lifelong learning and recreation and outstanding opportunities for collaborative research and development. In today's knowledge-based economy, the city's college, university and schools are key factors for success. ◄

(above) The UWO campus features a "Collegiate Gothic" style of architecture that contrasts with Fanshawe College's modern architecture. Despite the schools' varying architectural styles, there is increasing cooperation between the two institutions to respond to the changing environment for their graduates. Photo by Mike Grandmaison.

(left) UWO's Richard Ivey School of Business is an integral part of the university and is ranked among the best business schools in the world. Photo by Mike Grandmaison.

(left) Like Fanshawe, Western's campus is a resource for the people of Southwestern Ontario, providing a wide range of continuing education offerings, both on campus and via distance education, as well as recreational opportunities including theatre, visual arts, music and sports. Photo by Mike Grandmaison.

(below) The presence of a strong educational community improves the overall quality of life in London by fostering an atmosphere of growth, a willingness to learn, and by providing a strong and ready workforce. Photo by Mike Grandmaison.

Feeling Better Already

Londoners like having access to world-class care and they can see the potential for important economic spin-offs. In a remarkable vote of confidence, the London City Council made a $15 million commitment toward the cost of hospital restructuring in June 1999. Pictured is the garden at Parkwood Hospital, a rehabilitation, geriatrics, and complex-care hospital that is a part of the St. Joseph's Health Centre network. Photo by Mike Grandmaison.

I n January 1999, a quiet event on Canada's Pacific coast riveted the attention of land-locked Londoners.

That was the day that John Davidson completed his 8,300 kilometre journey by foot across Canada to raise money for research into genetic disease. Jesse's Journey, A Father's Tribute, as his heroic effort was called, began six months earlier on a windswept shore in Newfoundland. As Davidson made his way across Canada, Londoners watched his progress with anxious pride. It ended when he dipped his feet into the Pacific Ocean.

Davidson was inspired by his 18-year-old son Jesse, who has Duchenne Muscular Dystrophy. He began his fund raising efforts in 1995, by walking across Ontario with Jesse in his wheelchair. The cross-country journey was designed to raise money and public awareness, but it also raised hopes and hearts.

In many respects, London is the natural home for a project like Jesse's Journey. The city has an exceptionally strong health care and research sector, with two teaching hospitals, a medical school, the Canadian Medical Hall of Fame and several nationally recognized research institutes. London's hospitals alone account for 13 per cent of the city's tax revenues and support 22,400 jobs directly or indirectly in the local economy.

Londoners like having access to world class care and they can see the potential for important economic spin-offs. In a remarkable vote of confidence, London City Council made a $15 million commitment toward the cost of hospital restructuring in June 1999.

The city has a proud tradition of excellence in medicine. Sir Frederick Banting, co-discoverer of insulin, was a lecturer at the university's Medical School. While studying up for a lecture on carbohydrate metabolism, Banting had the idea that led to the discovery of insulin. Today, London researchers lead the search for a cure for Type 1 Diabetes.

Banting is not London's only medical superman, however. Dr. Murray Barr, also a member of the medical faculty, discovered the "sex chromatin," a genetic marker later known as the Barr Body, at Western in 1948. The Barr Body opened the way to new knowledge about the relationship between abnormalities in sex chromosomes and human disease. The "cobalt bomb" was developed at Western and first used at Victoria Hospital (now London Health Sciences Centre). London doctors Noble and Beer developed "vinblastine," one of the first effective anti-cancer drugs.

In more recent years, Dr. Charles Drake, a London neurosurgeon, pioneered techniques of surgical intervention for the treatment of cerebral aneurysms and Dr. Henry Barnett established the usefulness of aspirin for the prevention of debilitating effects of stroke. It was in London that the first Canadian heart transplant was performed in 1981, the first human image was produced in Canada using Magnetic Resonance Imaging in 1982, and the world's first pacemaker defibrillator was implanted in 1987. In 1988, a London

The history of St. Joseph's Health Centre began with the arrival of the Sisters of St. Joseph in London in 1869, and the opening of a 10-bed hospital in 1888. Over the years, the hospital continued to expand, and in 1983 the Lawson Research Institute was formed to support the hospital's growing clinical research program. In 1985, the boards of St. Joseph's Hospital and St. Mary's Hospital, a long-term care facility, merged to form St. Joseph's Health Centre. Photo by Mike Grandmaison.

surgical team performed the world's first successful small bowel transplant and in 1993, the same team performed the country's first pediatric liver transplant.

Building on this tradition, the city's health sector is now in the process of restructuring to meet the needs of the new millennium. Each component of today's complex system has its roots in London's past.

The history of St. Joseph's Health Centre began with the arrival of the Sisters of St. Joseph in London in 1869. Commissioned to visit the sick and poor, teach the young and open an orphanage, the Sisters expanded their mandate by opening a ten-bed hospital in 1888. By 1892, the Sisters had built an elegant new three-storey building on the current site to house the growing hospital.

The hospital continued to expand with the city it served. In 1983 the Lawson Research Institute was formed to support the hospital's growing clinical research program. In 1985 the boards of St. Joseph's Hospital and St. Mary's Hospital, a long-term care facility, merged to form St. Joseph's Health Centre. In 1997 Parkwood Hospital, a rehabilitation, geriatrics and complex care hospital in London's south end, joined the centre, and the following year, it took on responsibility for the management and governance of the London and St. Thomas Psychiatric Hospitals. Today, the hospital enjoys a national reputation in fields such as neonatal care, hand and upper limb, care of the elderly and renal lithotripsy.

The story behind London Health Sciences Centre (LHSC) is even longer. The city had a woefully inadequate public hospital by the 1850s, but it was not until 1875 that London General Hospital was built on a site overlooking the south bank of the Thames river. In 1899, the hospital was expanded significantly and renamed to honor Queen Victoria. The building with its distinctive bell tower was a

London has a proud tradition of excellence in medicine. Sir Frederick Banting, co-discoverer of insulin, was a lecturer at the university's medical school. While studying for a lecture on carbohydrate metabolism Banting had the idea that led to the discovery of insulin. Today, London researchers lead the search for a cure for Type 1 diabetes. Banting is honored at the Banting National Historic Site. Photo by Mike Grandmaison.

local landmark for decades. Eventually the riverside site became overcrowded and in the early 1970s, construction of a new hospital complex began further south.

In 1972 University Hospital, conveniently located adjacent to the university's medical school, was opened by Dr. Wilder Penfield. The new hospital quickly established an international reputation in the field of transplantation and stroke and cardiac care.

In 1995 the boards of the two hospitals, recognizing the inefficiency of having two similar acute care hospitals in the same community, reached agreement to merge as London Health Sciences Centre. Today, London Health Sciences Centre, which includes the Children's Hospital of Western Ontario and partners closely with the London Regional Cancer Clinic, treats more than 700,000 patients annually. It is renowned for a variety of programs, including groundbreaking robot-assisted minimally-invasive cardiac surgery and the world-famous Multi-Organ Transplant unit.

London's hospital sector is undergoing major changes, the result, in part, of the provincial government's overall health care restructuring program. Under the new plan, St. Joseph's Health Centre will focus

on long-term care of the elderly and mentally ill and ambulatory care (day and short-stay surgery and out-patient clinics). London Health Sciences Centre, consolidated on two campuses, will become the region's acute care hospital. The original riverside site will be abandoned. Emergency and critical care will be delivered at both sites, with most other care programs at one site. The London and St. Thomas Psychiatric Hospitals will eventually be closed and a new facility created under the auspices of the St. Joseph's Health Centre. Both hospitals will work closely to create a continuum of care for patients. While these changes are being made, the hospitals will also update and modernize their equipment and physical facilities. The total cost of restructuring is estimated at more than $300 million, with $120 million to be raised privately.

London also has a long tradition of medical education. It was in 1882 that instruction began at the Western Medical School, housed in a five-room cottage on the grounds of a former boys' school. The school continued to operate, even when the university's arts faculty was closed for lack of funds between 1885 to 1895. For many years, the school was located in a building close to Victoria Hospital. In

(above) The Robarts Research Institute, located on the campus of the University of Western Ontario adjacent to University Hospital, is Canada's only privately operated research institute. Robarts scientists work in eight areas, and the facility is renowned for its work in the development of 3D imaging. Photo by Mike Grandmaison.

(below) London's emphasis on health care and health research assures that a wide range of state-of-the-art medical facilities and expert medical personnel is available to its population. Photo by Mike Grandmaison.

1965, it moved to a new building on the main campus of the university at the north end of the city. A few years later, work began on the adjacent hospital and the School of Dentistry. Today, the faculty of Medicine and Dentistry offers undergraduate, graduate and continuing education. The Faculty recently introduced an innovative new problem-based curriculum.

London's outstanding research institutes were outgrowths of the hospitals and medical school. The Lawson Research Institute, for example, was founded in 1983 at St. Joseph's Hospital with the support of the Sisters of St. Joseph. Perhaps best known internationally for its work in the field of fetal and neonatal studies, the institute also has groups in molecular medicine, musculoskeletal research, general clinical research, imaging and rehabilitation and geriatric care. Lawson has been involved in several major clinical trials, including Aricept, a new drug to treat Alzhemer's Disease, and acarbose, a medication developed to improve blood sugar levels in patients with Type Two Diabetes.

The Robarts Research Institute, Canada's only privately-operated research institute, was established on the campus of the University of Western Ontario, adjacent to University Hospital, in 1986. Robarts scientists work in eight areas: autoimmunity/diabetes, clinical pharmacology, clinical trials, gene therapy and molecular virology, heart and circulation, imaging research, stroke and neurodegenerative disorders and transplantation and immunobiology. World-renowned for its work in the development of 3D imaging, the institute is home to a 4-Tesla Functional Magnetic Resonance Imaging unit, one of a handful in the world.

The Siebens-Drake Research Institute is a joint agricultural and medical research facility operated by Agriculture and Agri-Food Canada, the London Health Sciences Centre, the University of Western Ontario and the Robarts Research Institute. SDRI researchers have discovered that tobacco leaves can be used to produce enzymes that may prevent diabetes or treat Crohn's disease. In September 1999, the Institute hosted a major international conference on molecular farming.

London Health Sciences Centre also has an extensive research capability, administered through Research Inc., a non-share capital company. Researchers at LHSC attract $25 million in annual funding. The centre has some 350 ongoing clinical trials, including the only Canadian node in a project studying cartilage transplantation for the treatment of some forms of arthritis.

The strength of London's medical research sector is reflected in the key role its members played in the development of the recently-created Canadian Institutes of Health Research, which were also strongly supported by the city's Chamber of Commerce. Extraordinary concentration of research excellence is a great lifestyle advantage for Londoners, ensuring that they receive the most advanced medical care available. But it also provides a platform for economic growth. Advances and discoveries in research institutes often lead to commercialization and to the development of successful companies.

London's researchers have already spawned several promising young companies, including:
• Viron Therapeutics Inc., which conducts early stage development of therapeutic proteins from viral sources
• EVS Enhanced Vision Systems, which is developing a number of applications for advanced Computed Tomography (CT) imaging
• Life Imaging Systems Inc., founded to further develop the

innovative 3-dimensional ultrasound technology developed at Robarts Research Institute

- London Clinical Trials Research Group, an academic contract research organization
- Diabetogen, a biopharmaceutical company focused on discovering and developing new chemicals and biologicals for the prevention and treatment of Type I Diabetes
- Medprep, a joint venture between London Health Sciences Centre and Oxoid Inc. to manufacture culture media for use in the fields of microbiology, virology and immunology
- Sonometrics, which produces a sophisticated ultrasound measurement device

Many Londoners are convinced that the economic potential of the biotech sector is enormous. The head office of Canadian Medical Discoveries Fund Inc. is located in London. CMDF, a venture capital investment fund focusing on the life sciences industry, was founded in 1994 and has since attracted assets of more than $240 million. Dr. Calvin Stiller, a leading London surgeon and researcher, provides leadership to the Fund. More recently, several groups have come together to develop plans for the London Biotechnology Incubator, which will help young biotech companies establish viable businesses.

(above) London's hospitals account for 13 per cent of the city's tax revenues and support 22,400 jobs directly or indirectly in the local economy, benefiting the area's overall quality of life. Photo by Mike Grandmaison.

(left) The Siebens-Drake Research Institute is a joint agricultural and medical research facility operated by Agriculture and Agri-Food Canada, the London Health Sciences Centre, the University of Western Ontario, and the Robarts Research Institute. SDRI researchers have discovered that tobacco leaves can be used to produce enzymes that may prevent diabetes or treat Crohn's disease. Photo by Mike Grandmaison.

One of the most powerful symbols of London's stature as a medical centre is its choice as the location of the Canadian Medical Hall of Fame. Launched in 1994, the Hall celebrates the careers of distinguished scientists and physicians, including Doctors Best and Banting, Dr. Wilder Penfield, Dr. Norman Bethune and Dr. Roberta Bondar. New laureates are selected and inducted every 18 months. Their photographs and stories are on display in a special gallery at the London Regional Art and Historical Museums.

Several London physicians, including Doctors Barnett and Barr, have already been inducted into the Hall, but many more will join its august ranks as London matures in its role as one of Canada's premier medical centres. ▮

E I G H T

Service With A Smile

London offers world-class shops, restaurants, entertainment, and sporting events. In 1998, visitors to London generated more than $400 million in economic activity. Photo by Mike Grandmaison.

T he merger of Canada Trust with the Toronto-Dominion Bank on February 1, 2000 had special meaning for Londoners. After all, it was in London that a group of local businessmen founded the Huron and Erie Savings and Loan Society, the forerunner of Canada Trust, in 1864.

London is a shopper's paradise, with more than its share of retail businesses. Richmond Row is a string of specialty shops, restaurants, and pubs located north of the downtown along several blocks of the city's main north-south artery. Photo by Mike Grandmaison.

From those small beginnings, London grew into a national center for financial services. Today, although the financial services sector is not as dominant as it once was, service remains central to the London economy. In addition to banks and insurance companies, the city has a vibrant retail sector and is becoming an attractive convention and tourism center.

Founded as an alternative to 19th century "loan sharks," Canada Trust grew steadily, eventually bringing together more than 50 mortgage, loan, trust and real estate companies under its banner and expanding across Canada. By 1998, the company controlled corporate assets of nearly $50 billion. Although Canada Trust maintained a dual head office presence in Toronto and London from the early '60s, many major national operations remained in London, including systems programming, MasterCard and collections. Canada Trust was an innovator in telephone and electronic banking, establishing a 24-hour a day call center in London in the mid-'90s. The newly merged organization has pledged that it will maintain 3,200 employees in London.

Only ten years after the formation of the Huron and Erie, London saw the founding of another financial services giant, the London Life Insurance Company. Again, it was a local success story that became a national force, eventually Canada's largest provider of life insurance. The London Life Freedom 55™ brand remains one of the most recognized and successful in the industry. In 1997 London Life became part of the Great West Life Assurance Company. The company maintains a significant operation in London, headquartered in a stately 1927 building (famous for its emerald-green lawn) overlooking Victoria Park.

Nearly a century later, London birthed a third national financial services company. Avco Financial Services was launched in 1954 with an investment of $25,000 from two partners, an appliance store owner and a commercial market gardener. The company developed branches across Canada before being purchased in 1999 by The Associates, a U.S.-based company that provides consumer finance and other financial services. London remains home office for The Associates consumer lending operation in Canada.

The smallest of London's homegrown financial services organizations is St. Willibrord Community Credit Union. Launched in 1951 to serve the social and financial needs of the many Dutch and Flemish immigrants in southwestern Ontario, St. Willibrord's now has more than 30,000 members throughout the region.

In addition to London-born organizations, the city has regional offices and multiple branches of the major banks, including Royal Bank, Canadian Imperial Bank of Commerce, Bank of Nova Scotia and Bank of Montreal.

London is a shopper's paradise, with more than its share of retail businesses. Like most major North America cities, London's retail sector is anchored by major suburban malls each with some 200 stores. Whiteoaks Mall dominates in the south, Westmount in the west and Masonville Place in the north. Both Whiteoaks and Masonville are surrounded by mushrooming "big box" developments. A number of smaller malls and plazas serve specific city neighborhoods. Cherryhill Village Mall, for example, accurately reflects the nature of the surrounding community, mostly apartments rented by retirees.

Galleria London, the city's downtown mall, has struggled to compete with the free parking and convenient locations of the suburban malls. It lost an important tenant when the Eaton's store closed in the fall of 1999 and another when The Bay moved out in early 2000. Selected as the site for the new public library, the Galleria is gradually being reborn as an integral part of the downtown community.

London also has several distinctive street-level shopping districts. Richmond Row is a string of specialty shops, restaurants and pubs located north of the downtown along several blocks of the city's main north-south artery. Wortley Village, just south of downtown, is a two-block commercial district that has long served the close-knit neighborhood of Old South but is now becoming a chic shopping destination. Hamilton Road is dotted with small shops that reflect the city's growing ethnic diversity. An interesting collection of shops and restaurants is also developing around the new $14-million Covent Garden market.

The city's two most distinctive and historic stores are both located downtown. Kingsmill's, a department store founded on Dundas Street in 1865, is still run by the great-grandson of the founder. Although the merchandise is modern and upscale, Kingsmill's features tin ceilings, hardwood floors, a hand-driven elevator and an old-fashioned emphasis on customer service. A block east of Kingsmill's is Nash Jewellers, established by the grandfather of the current owner in 1918. The store's elegant façade has come to represent quality and expertise to generations of Londoners.

Great shopping is just one reason London is becoming a favorite convention destination. The city also offers uncrowded streets, excellent hotels and a world-class convention center. Completed in 1993 at a cost of $40 million, the centre is owned by the City of London. It hosts national conventions and conferences, social events such as large dinners and trade and consumer shows. Among the high-profile events held at the London Convention Centre are: the PC Party of Ontario Convention (1994, 1997), the Liberal Party of Ontario Convention (1994, 1995, 1999), the Assembly of First Nations (1996), the Canadian Diabetes Association Annual Meeting (1997)

Once thought of as relatively unadventurous in cuisine, London now offers a range of restaurant choices from English-style to Italian, Greek, Eastern European, Indian, Thai, and Vietnamese cuisine. Photo by Mike Grandmaison.

(top) Today, London remains a national center for financial services. It has seen the founding of national giants including London Life Insurance Company, which would become Canada's largest provider of life insurance. Photo by Mike Grandmaison.

(above) Learning and entertainment combine in the magical shows offered at London's IMAX theatre. Photo by Mike Grandmaison.

and the Reform Party of Canada National Convention (1998). In 2002, London will also host the Canadian Chamber of Commerce Convention.

The facilities of the Convention Centre are complemented by a variety of smaller venues throughout the city, including The University of Western Ontario, Spencer Hall Conference Centre and the Four Points Hotel Sheraton. The city has more than 30 hotels, motels and inns, including a Hilton, a Delta and a Radisson. Once thought of as relatively unadventurous in cuisine, London now offers a range of restaurant choices from English-style to Italian, Greek, Eastern European, Indian, Thai and Vietnamese cuisine.

Although much of London's charm lies in its quiet, leafy neighborhoods and parks, the city also has a number of major tourist attractions. For those with a taste for the past, there's Eldon House, an elegant early 19th century house set in beautiful grounds; the Old Courthouse and Gaol; Fanshawe Pioneer Village, a living history museum; the London Museum of Archaeology, which includes a reconstructed 500-year-old Neutral Iroquoian village; Banting House, which commemorates the achievements of Sir Frederick Banting, co-discoverer of insulin; the Royal Canadian Regiment Museum, featuring memorabilia of the famous regiment; and the Guy Lombardo Museum, which remembers one of the city's most famous sons.

London has a special appeal for children. More than 40 years ago, the Public Utilities Commission opened Storybook Gardens, a small zoo in an imaginative storybook setting created in a corner of Springbank Park. The attraction opened with an unplanned publicity stunt: one of two sea lions flown in from California escaped into the Thames River. "Slippery," as he was quickly dubbed, made it all the way to Sandusky, Ohio, before being recaptured. He was returned with great fanfare by officials of the Toledo zoo and tens of thousands of Londoners turned out to watch his entourage pass. Today, Storybook Gardens remains a popular destination, often combined with a trip on the miniature diesel railway and a turn on the vintage merry-go-round just outside its gates. Young visitors to London also enjoy the London Regional Children's Museum, which offers a "hands-on approach to learning" and the London International Children's Festival held each June. For more active family times, East Park Golf Gardens, Wally World, Laser Quest and Cosmo City offer everything from go-karting and waterslides to laser tag and arcade machines. During the summer, the London Princess offers river cruises and a double-decker bus tours the city.

Sport tourism brings thousands of visitors to London each year. The London Gus Macker three-on-three basketball tournament, held in Victoria Park each May, is one of the largest in Canada. The city also has excellent facilities for baseball and soccer tournaments and is building two major new hockey arenas. For those who prefer spectator sports, the London Knights hockey team and the London Werewolves baseball team provide excitement. The Canadian Baseball Hall of Fame is located in St. Mary's, a half-hour drive from London. During a single weekend in early September 1999, soccer and baseball tournaments attracted 14,000 visitors to the city and added an estimated $2.7 million to the regional economy.

London's summer festivals are also magnets for tourists. With something planned for almost every weekend from late May to early

Modern shopping centers offer convenient access to a wide variety of choices in food, clothing, entertainment, and other consumer goods. Photo by Mike Grandmaison.

London offers a world-class convention centre, completed in 1993 at a cost of $40 million. The Centre is owned by the City of London and hosts national conventions and conferences, social events such as large dinners, and trade and consumer shows. Photo by Mike Grandmaison.

Galleria London, the city's downtown mall, has been selected as the site for the new public library, sparking its rebirth as an integral part of the downtown community. Photo by Mike Grandmaison.

Special events such as the London Balloon Festival and Rib-Fest, held in August, draw thousands of visitors to the city every year. Photo by Mike Grandmaison.

September, the events range from a major air show in June to the famous Home Country Folk Festival in July and the London Balloon Festival and Rib-Fest in August.

London's growing tourism industry is overseen by Tourism London, an innovative private-public partnership with a membership of more than 200 businesses. Strategic direction is provided by a Board of Directors drawn from the local hospitality and tourism industry. Sports tourism and special events have been identified as an important focus for the organization. In 1998, visitors to London generated more than $400 million in economic activity.

Another attraction that brings many visitors to London each year is the Western Fair. Founded in 1867, the Western Fair Association began life as an agricultural society responsible for mounting an annual fall fair. Today, the 10-day fair is still popular, attracting 300,000 visitors and generating $3 million in revenues. The association also operates the 66-acre fair site year-round, offering horse racing, slot machine gambling, dining, banquet facilities, dozens of consumer and trade shows and an IMAX theatre. ▮

The first in a series of major downtown building projects—a new farmer's market—opened with great fanfare in October 1999. The striking red brick and glass Covent Garden Market building, which carries faint echoes of the original 1850s marketplace, offers produce, baked goods, meat, cheese, prepared foods, and crafts. The area around the market is alive with restaurants, pubs, and new retail stores. Photos by Mike Grandmaison.

(above) Like most major North American cities, London's retail sector is anchored by major suburban malls, each with some two hundred stores. Whiteoaks Mall (pictured) dominates in the south, Westmount in the west, and Masonville Place in the north. Photo by Mike Grandmaison.

(left) Kingsmill's, a department store founded on Dundas street in 1865, is still run by the great-grandson of the founder and features modern, upscale merchandise in an historic setting with tin ceilings, hardwood floors, a hand-driven elevator, and an old-fashioned emphasis on customer service. Photo by Mike Grandmaison.

(above) *The Covent Garden Market offers the region's finest fresh produce for choosy shoppers. Photo by Mike Grandmaison.*

(right) *The Western Fair, founded in 1867, draws 300,000 visitors and generates $3 million in revenue each year. Photo by Mike Grandmaison.*

(left) London has more than thirty hotels, motels, and inns, including a Hilton, a Delta (pictured), and a Radisson. Photo by Mike Grandmaison.

(right) The London Regional Children's Museum offers a "hands-on" approach to learning. Photo by Mike Grandmaison.

(below) London's growing tourism industry is overseen by Tourism London, an innovative private-public partnership with a membership of more than 200 businesses. Included in the events that draw visitors to London annually is the Western Fair, which features food, entertainment, rides, games, and more. Photo by Mike Grandmaison.

Heart of the City

*The original Grand Theatre opened as the Grand Opera House in 1901.
Today, the Grand Theatre is one of Canada's leading regional theatres,
producing a season of major productions from September to May. Photo by
Marc MacBain, Sudden Exposure.*

I	magine a lovely spring evening in London, Ontario. At the London Regional Art and Historical Museums, a group of art enthusiasts stroll in a gallery overlooking the Thames River, viewing a new exhibit of contemporary paintings. A few blocks east, the lights dim and the curtain rises on a Grand Theatre production. Across Victoria Park from the theatre, the thrilling sound of an orchestra tuning signals the beginning of another Orchestra London concert.

Here, within a radius of less than a mile, are London's three major arts organizations. If the arts are truly the heart of any community, the city's pulse is strong in these few blocks.

There is another sense in which these three important institutions are the heart of the city: they are all part of London's downtown. Once a vibrant retail and business community, London's core has suffered from the malaise affecting many North American cities. But thanks to a concerted effort by city government and citizens, the downtown is coming back to life.

London has had a strong arts community since the 1880s, when the Western Art League was formed. In the early years, exhibits were held at the public library and at the annual agricultural fair. In 1940 the London Art Gallery was opened on the second floor of the new public library on Queen's Avenue, where among other innovative programs, it began renting art. By the '60s it was clear that more space was needed, but it wasn't until 1980 that the new gallery, designed by renowned architect Raymond Moriyama, was opened at a site overlooking the Forks of the Thames. The art gallery was eventually merged with the city's historical museum administration, taking over operation of Eldon House, home of one of London's first families. Each year, the London Regional Art and Historical Museums mounts dozens of art and museum exhibitions, and sponsors film showings, courses, special events and children's programs.

At roughly the same time the new gallery was under way, the Grand Theatre was also undergoing major reconstruction. The original theatre opened as the Grand Opera House on September 9, 1901. During its first 75 years, the Grand's stage was graced by such famous figures as pianist Jan Paderewski and actors Sarah Bernhardt, Bela Lugosi, Jessica Tandy, John Gilegud, Sidney Poitier and Frederick March. After a short stint as a movie theatre and a longer period in the hands of an amateur group, the Grand became a fully professional theatre in 1971. A few years later, the decision was taken to rebuild the theatre, retaining the elaborately painted proscenium arch but little else. Today, the Grand Theatre is one of Canada's leading regional theatres, producing a season of major productions from September to May. A small studio theatre, the McManus, presents a varied program,

Art doesn't always have to be serious, as this whimsical statue of Humpty Dumpty (presumably before his "great fall") in Storybook Gardens goes to prove. Photo by Mike Grandmaison.

including children's and experimental theatre. Despite the usual financial challenges that face most regional theatres, the Grand continues to be a favorite destination for Londoners.

Orchestra London, which celebrated its 50th anniversary in 1999, is another exceptional cultural resource for a city the size of London. Nationally renowned, the ensemble is frequently broadcast by CBC Radio and has recorded three compact discs. Like the theatre, Orchestra London has had its financial ups and downs but continues to attract enthusiastic audiences. The season of classical and popular concerts runs from October to May, and include such perennial favorites as "Jeans and Classics," music of the '60s, '70s and '80s in an informal nightclub setting, and "Cushion Concerts" for children two to six.

A fourth cultural landmark located in London's heart is the London Public Library. A valued part of city life for more than 100 years, the LPL has been headquartered in an impressive Depression-era building on Queens Avenue that is now bursting at the seams. The library's board has decided to expand and to move the operation to the renovated former Bay store in Galleria London, the city's downtown mall. The library operates 14 branches in various parts of the city, with a total circulation of more than 3.5 million. The branches also offer author readings, book groups, concerts, lectures, courses and programs for children.

London's daily newspaper, the *London Free Press*, is another important component of the city's cultural life. Established in 1849 by Scottish-born printer William Sutherland, the paper was owned and operated for many years by the Blackburn family. The Blackburns eventually owned local AM and FM radio stations and a television station as well. Since the sudden death of Martha Blackburn in 1992, the other media outlets have been sold off and the newspaper has become part of the Sun Media empire. It continues to put a strong emphasis on community service and local news. Bowes Publishing, a 50-year-old newspaper and magazine publisher that once competed with the Blackburn Group, is now also owned by Sun Media. Bowes produces the *Business London* magazine, among other publications. *Scene Magazine*, an arts and entertainment tabloid continues to present a refreshingly offbeat take on the city's cultural scene.

The downtown has no monopoly on arts and culture. There are cultural groups and arts organizations located in every corner of the city. The dance scene ranges from Morris and Scottish Country to ballet and Middle Eastern. Musical groups include the Amabile Singers, the Canadian Welsh Singers, the Gerald Fagan singers, the Karen Schuessler Singers, London Pro Musica and the London Fanshawe Symphonic Chorus. Musical ensembles include Scottish and Irish pipe bands, brass, percussion and Baroque instruments. London also has a vibrant amateur theatre community led by the London Community Players, which operates a 355-seat theatre in east London. Private art galleries abound.

Arts festivals fill the London calendar from spring until fall. The Home County Folk Festival, for example, has been held in July at Victoria Park for more than 25 years. The London International

Children's Festival brings performers from around the world to London for a week of performances in June. In September, the London New Arts Festivals provides a venue for musicians, writers, painters and dancers on the leading edge of contemporary culture. Panorama and Sunfest International Music Festival celebrate London's growing ethnic diversity.

Despite the bright spots, London's downtown, like that of many North American cities, has languished over the past three decades, with the move to suburban housing developments and malls. The large downtown mall built in the late '80s, Galleria London, failed to lure the promised crowds. But the tide is clearly turning. For several years, Londoners have discussed ways to rejuvenate the city's core. In early 1998, a group of concerned citizens and City councilors formed the Downtown Millennium Plan Committee and developed a five-year plan of potential capital projects and other initiatives.

To support its work, the City of London has developed several

The art that abounds throughout the city is evident even in the architecture of London, as in this architectural detail from the historic public library building. Photo by Mike Grandmaison.

downtown development incentives, including façade restoration loan programs and density bonuses. In late 1999, it hosted a team of planners from the "National Main Street Centre" in Washington, D.C., which has successfully steered core revitalization in several U.S. cities. Suggestions now being implemented include more free parking, active business recruitment to the core, façade restoration, residential development and more.

The first in a series of major downtown building projects—a new farmer's market—opened with great fanfare in October 1999. The striking red brick and glass building, which carries faint echoes of the original 1850s marketplace, offers produce, baked goods, meat, cheese, prepared foods and crafts. The area around the Covent Garden market is alive with restaurants, pubs and new retail stores.

Another major project is the new hockey arena and entertainment complex under construction on the near-empty block opposite the market. This piece of land once contained a handsome Victorian streetscape, demolished to make way for a shopping mall that was never built. The new facility, designed to incorporate the one surviving 19th century building, will be the new home of the city's OHL team.

Other downtown developments include handsome new entrances to Victoria Park, improvements to the parkland at the Forks of the Thames, better lighting, surveillance cameras and landscaping. Soon the geographic heart of London will beat with as much vigor as its cultural one. ⁍

Independent artists are encouraged to display their talents - whether through music, visual or performing arts—at the many fairs and festivals held throughout the year. Photo courtesy Tourism London.

Photo by Mike Grandmaison.

Each year, the London Regional Art and Historical Museums mounts dozens of exhibitions and sponsors film showings, courses, special events, and children's programs. Photo by Mike Grandmaison.

Some art is less than subtle. Museum visitors can't help but notice, nor easily forget, this striking rhinoceros sculpture standing guard beside the building. Photo by Mike Grandmaison.

CHAPTER

TEN

Room to Grow

Photo by Mike Grandmaison

S eptember 8, 1999. Labatt Park in downtown London. Ninth inning of the Frontier Baseball League championship game. London Werewolves up 4-1.

Their opponents, the Chilicothe Paints, have two men on and the tying run at the plate. The batter hits a long ball toward the gap between centre and right centre field. With the crowd of more than 3,500 on its feet, the Werewolves' right fielder chases the ball down and makes a great catch. The game is over. The championship belongs to the Werewolves.

Photo by Mike Grandmaison

It was a moment of pure euphoria for London baseball fans. The Werewolves, playing their first season in London, had exceeded all expectations, producing a season of entertaining and winning baseball.

It was just one more chapter in London's long love affair with baseball. Played in the city since the 1850s, baseball was given a permanent home with the building of a ballpark at the Forks of the Thames in 1877. That year, the London Tecumsehs, the city's first professional team, won their league championships, thanks in large part to the curve ball invented by pitcher Fred Goldsmith. Tecumseh Park, later renamed Labatt Park to honor the generous support of the brewery, is the oldest ballpark in continuous use in Canada.

Labatt Park is just one of the many beautiful parks in London—active spaces with excellent facilities for sports and cool green oases that are suited for walking, biking or simply existing peacefully. The city's nickname, "The Forest City," was originally a reference to the fact that pioneer London was a clearing in primal forest. Today it honors the many open spaces and shady boulevards.

London's first park was dedicated by Lord Dufferin, the Governor General of Canada, in August 1874. Until 1868 the land had been part of the British garrison, a dusty, treeless parade ground surrounded by a rustic stump fence. When the garrison was withdrawn, a London councilor lobbied the federal government for a portion of the land as a park. His request was granted and the park was designed, laid out and planted. Today, Victoria Park is a much-loved downtown green space, the site of several summer festivals and the traditional Winter Wonderland display of colored lights. The park is currently undergoing a redevelopment plan that will support its use for festivals while preserving its tranquil atmosphere. The City of London recently gave it a heritage designation, appropriate recognition of its role in city life for 125 years.

Another early park in London was the unintended side effect of the city's first waterworks. In the late 1870s, the city bought a piece of land on the Thames River west of the city. The land was well supplied with natural springs to supply pure water, and had a steep hill nearby, the perfect site for a gravity-feed reservoir. But the area was also very scenic. Before long, picnics at Waterworks Park became a London tradition. In the early days, the roads were terrible, but the park could be reached by a pleasant steamer trip from the Forks of the Thames. Later, visitors traveled to the park by an open-sided streetcar.

Reservoir Park, now called Springbank, has remained a favorite with Londoners. Today, it features a charming mini-zoo, a miniature diesel train, a vintage merry-go-round and many acres of peaceful riverside meadows.

While Victoria and Springbank remain the jewels in London's crown of parks, there are more than 200 parks and open spaces in the city, covering some 5,000 hectares. In recent years, many of them have been linked by a riverside bike and walking path that meanders along both the north and south branches of the Thames, meets at the Forks in downtown London, and continues as far as Springbank Park in the west. Plans call for the paths to be extended in the future, creating a city-wide network of green spaces.

In addition to manicured parks and playing fields, the city has designated several Environmentally Significant Areas, including the Sifton Bog, Warbler Woods, Westminster Ponds, Meadowlily Woods and the Medway Valley. These areas, home to rare plants and wildlife, are preserved in their natural state. Walking paths and boardwalks provide public access without disturbing the delicate balance of nature.

There are some 130 neighborhood parks in London, many of them strongly supported by their local communities. Planning regulations call for at least five per cent of the land in any new development to be set aside for park use, so that the system continues to grow with the city. Innovative private-public partnerships help fund facilities in these parks. For example, the local Saturn dealership donated play structures to two neighborhood parks in 1998 and 1999, while a McDonalds restaurant contributed to a third.

Ninety years ago, the City began offering summer playground programs in neighborhood parks. Today, the Department of Recreation and Community Programs offers dozens of activities on a year-round basis—everything from neighborhood day camps, tennis lessons and leadership camps to Tai Chi, meditation and ceramics. Almost 4,000 Londoners participate in adult sport leagues and some 25,000 take swimming lessons.

The Department pays special attention to the needs of special groups. It has a financial assistance policy to ensure that people with disabilities can participate fully in recreational programs, and special programming to encourage girls and women to remain active in sports and to foster participation among people from ethnic communities. In addition to city-sponsored recreation, a number of volunteer and for-profit groups organize baseball, hockey, soccer and basketball teams throughout the city.

London boasts three public indoor pools, 35 outdoor pools and wading pools, 11 arenas and 10 community centres. The newest indoor pool, the South London Community Pool, was completed in late 1998 at a cost of $3.8 million. Three senior community centres offer a wide range of programs, including excursions, entertainment, crafts and sports. At the other end of the age spectrum, one of the city's newest and most unusual facilities is a skateboard park, built, like Victoria Park, on the land of a former military base. Privately owned facilities like Wally World, a large water park, and East Park Golf Gardens, with a golf course, waterslide, go-karts and batting cages, offer more family fun.

Along with baseball, Londoners have a passion for golf. It is estimated that 42 per cent of men and 18 per cent of women in

Photos by Mike Grandmaison

London golf—almost twice the Canadian and Ontario averages. London was one of the first cities in eastern Canada to establish a municipal golf course.

The concept was championed by Dr. E.V. Buchanan, a Scottish engineer who became General Manager of the city's Public Utilities Commission. Buchanan was impressed by the number of municipal courses in Britain and decided London needed something similar. In 1922, he raised the money for the first nine holes by selling memberships to the non-existent club. Buchanan was also the prime mover behind the development of city-run recreation programs. "A sound body," he once wrote in a PUC annual report, "is the first requisite of good citizenship."

There are now three city-owned courses, Thames Valley, Fanshawe and River Road. The city's Parkside Nine, which opened in 1998 adjacent to the Fanshawe course, is the first golf course in North America specifically designed for the physically challenged.

In addition to the city-owned courses, there are more than 30 private and public golf clubs in the London area. Among them is the London Hunt and Country Club, which has been the site for the Canadian Open, and Redtail, a privately-owned club whose owners have hosted Queen Elizabeth, actor Sean Connery and golfer Nick Price, among other celebrities.

Fanshawe Lake, formed by the construction of a dam on the River Thames, provides a close-to-home venue for sailing. London sailors also have access to excellent sailing on Lake Huron and Lake Erie, less than an hour's drive away. Fanshawe is also the main training site in Eastern Canada for Canada's national rowing team. The London Canoe Club and the London Rowing Club, both located on the Thames near Springbank Park, support an active boating community. The city has two downhill ski hills within easy reach and several facilities catering to cross-country skiiers.

For those who prefer spectator sports, the London Werewolves, the London Knights, and the University of Western Ontario Mustang sport teams provide many opportunities to see outstanding young athletes. The Knights, London's OHL franchise since 1968, is strongly supported by Londoners—as witnessed by the excitement generated in 1999 when the team won their division and went on the play in the OHL finals. Among the many Knights alumni who have gone on to careers in the NHL are Darryl Sittler, Rob Ramage, Dino Ciccarelli, Brendan Shanahan and Brad Marsh. The team will soon have a new centrally-located arena, part of the city's downtown renewal project. The University maintains 35 different teams, ranging from track and field and hockey to tennis and rugby. A new stadium, constructed on Western's campus for the 2001 Canada Games, will also provide a home for the Mustang football team, which has a proud 70-year tradition. ◄

Photo by Mike Grandmaison

Photos by Mike Grandmaison

E P I L O G U E

What does a six-foot-tall red fox have to do with London's future?

As the official mascot of the 2001 Canada Summer Games, Waagosh the fox represents an innovative alliance of London and four community partners. The alliance worked together to win the bid to hold the Games, and to organize and market the event.

Alliances and partnerships are the way of the future, and this is just one example of London's talent for putting together powerful ones.

The Canada Summer Games will bring more than 4,000 of Canada's top young athletes, and some 30,000 spectators, to the London area for a two-week period in August 2001. The Games are expected to have an economic impact of $42-million on London, and create 571 jobs. When it's all over, the city will have a brand new stadium, an upgraded aquatic center and a $2-million endowment fund for amateur sport.

One key to the successful bid was London's alliance with The University of Western Ontario and the neighboring communities of St. Thomas, Woodstock and Grand Bend. It was a windy and wet day in May 1997 when the Games site selection committee visited the region. Despite the weather, enthusiastic crowds greeted the members of the committee wherever they went. This demonstration of community support, combined with strong leadership, a good financial plan and the powerful alliance, won the day.

The heart of the Games is The University of Western Ontario, where the athletes will be housed and most of the events take place. The brand new multi-use stadium being built for the Games will replace the University's aging J.W. Little Stadium. When the Games are over, the new stadium will become a resource to be shared by both the university and the community.

The Games are symbolic of a closer relationship between the university and the city. London's city council recently granted $10-million to the university to support its capital campaign, recognizing Western's important role in building the reputation of the city and contributing to its economic growth.

Another partnership is now promoting London's economic development. The London Economic Development Corporation (LEDC) is a non-profit corporation that brings together municipal government and local business. The formation of LEDC is the culmination of a process that began in the 1997 when a grassroots business organization called Advance London threw down a challenge to city government and the London community, calling for the "privatization" of economic development.

Advance London's arguments found a receptive ear at city hall, where a number of politicians were also wondering if London could do more to leverage its many business advantages. The City had some positive experience with private/public partnerships: in 1995 the Office of Visitors and Convention Services was transformed into Tourism London, a private agency composed mainly of representatives from the city's tourism and hospitality industry.

LEDC is overseen by a board of 17 Directors, 12 from the private sector and 5 appointed by City Council. The two-year-old organization has targeted six strategic sectors in which London has a competitive advantage: biotechnology, transportation, agri-business, manufacturing, telecommunications and information technology and financial services. Its long-term objectives are to attract new investment, retain and expand existing London businesses and market the strengths of London.

London's Chamber of Commerce has played a key role in London's new business-friendly approach. With 900 member firms employing 50,000 people in the London area, the Chamber has been very active in breaking down traditional barriers between the public and private sectors and creating common goals.

The Chamber played an important role as a broker between the city and the business community in the formation of the LEDC. It has also taken a proactive stance in the promotion of the NAFTA Superhighway. The Chamber is working actively to strengthen its ties with The University of Western Ontario, Fanshawe College, The Richard Ivey School of Business and *The London Free Press*.

The Chamber was also instrumental in the formation of The London Community Small Business Centre. The Centre, a partnership involving the Ontario Ministry of Economic Development, Trade and Tourism, the City of London, Bell Canada, the Canadian Imperial Bank of Commerce and the Canada Ontario Business Service Centre, supports the start-up and growth of small businesses. As well as information, counseling and mentoring, the Centre also assists entrepreneurs in identifying sources of financing. The Centre's business incubator leases space to start-up manufacturing businesses. Since 1986, more than 75 fledgling businesses have located in the incubator.

Another example of community partnership is London Venture Group Inc., a non-profit organization that matches local business people with investors. Volunteers from London's business community help young companies refine their business plans and identify the best sources of financing for their needs. LVG has facilitated more than $5-million in investments in about 20 companies during its five-year history. With the same focus on access to capital, Venture Capital London Inc. is a for-profit venture capital company that invests only in London and area companies. The group works closely with the LEDC, the Chamber, LVG and the Small Business Centre.

The London and District Labour Council, the voice of labour in London for more than 40 years, is also an important contributor to the community. Its members act as positive social advocates and volunteers in many organizations.

The City of London is an enthusiastic partner in all this activity to strengthen the city's business community. Apart from its involvement in LEDC and Tourism London, the city has signaled its "open for business" policy by freezing taxes for two years in a row, campaigning hard for the NAFTA superhighway and partnering in a number of major downtown projects. The City also moved quickly to implement many of the recommendations of the Small Business Task Force, making it easier and faster to apply for building permits, business licenses, severances and variances. The London Development Institute, the London Home Builders Association, the Chamber and the City Manager have established an innovative program to share concerns and issues around growth and development in the city. The "Old East Village" commercial district and the "Wellington Street Gateway," the main access route from Highway 401 to the downtown, have both been improved and beautified, and the unglamorous but essential task of upgrading the city's sewer system has begun. Council showed its faith in the city's biotech and health care sectors by making major contributions to the hospitals' capital campaigns and the building of the new biotech incubator.

Photo by Mark MacBain, Sudden Exposure

London has many economic and social advantages—its strategic location, vibrant business community, comfortable lifestyle, world class education and medical institutions and well-educated work force. But perhaps the most important driver of success is London's spirit of community co-operation. It was this spirit that gave birth to Waagosh the fox and the 2001 London Alliance. And it will be the driving force as London organizations forge new links at home and abroad. To be sure, London will stand out in the 21st century. But it will never stand alone. ⫶

part two

Photo by Mike Grandmaison

ELEVEN

Manufacturing and Distribution

Photo by Mike Grandmaison

ACCURIDE
CANADA INC.

C hances are the next heavy truck and trailer that rolls by is travelling on steel wheels made by the employees of Accuride Canada's plant in London, Ontario.

The Firestone Boulevard manufacturer annually produces about 5.5 million heavy and light wheels and rims for the North American market, in the largest commercial truck-wheel plant in the world. With more than 800 hourly and salaried employees, Accuride is London's fifth largest manufacturing employer. The hourly employees are represented by Local 27, Unit 17, of the Canadian Auto Workers.

Accuride Canada is a wholly-owned subsidiary of Accuride Corporation, which has its headquarters in Evansville, Indiana, and is part of North America's largest manufacturer and supplier of wheels for heavy and medium trucks and trailers. Besides the steel-wheel operations in London, Accuride has similar operations in Henderson, Kentucky; Columbia, Tennessee; and Monterrey, Mexico.

Accuride Corporation also produces aluminum wheels in Erie, Pennsylvania, and is involved in a commercial tire- and wheel-assembly joint venture in Springfield, Ohio, and Talbotville, Ontario. Besides trucks and trailers, the company produces wheels for buses, commercial light trucks and sport utility vehicles.

"North America mostly moves on Accuride wheels, and Accuride Canada is an important member of the total manufacturing team," says Stewart Doggett, Director of

A selection of light, medium and heavy wheels as manufactured at the London Plant.

Operations for the London plant. "Our people take great pride in the quality of their work. We're ISO 9001 and QS 9000 registered, meaning that our customers are assured excellent products, delivered on time, and often delivered by a truck mounted with Accuride-produced wheels."

"Each year we use more than 168,000 tons of steel produced in Canada by Algoma and Stelco," he continues, "so besides being a major provider of jobs in London, we make a significant contribution to the overall Canadian economy."

Accuride is a well-known name in London, where the company and its people take an active part in the community. It is also a company with a long legacy in the city, as its roots go back to The London & Petrolia Barrel Company, first established in 1886. Originally founded to serve the early Canadian oil industry in Petrolia and oil refineries in London, the company went on to produce a wide variety of wooden stave barrels for the food and beverage industry, and for a short period supplied barrels for the Canadian west coast whaling operations. As wooden barrels passed out of wide use, the company switched to production of stainless steel products, including beer kegs and premix tanks.

The original London & Petrolia Barrel Company plant was situated on Little Simcoe Street, and in 1950, it began producing truck wheels under license from Firestone Steel Products, a Division of The Firestone Tire and Rubber Company of Akron, Ohio. In 1968, Firestone acquired the "Barrel Works" and changed its name to Firestone Steel Products of Canada, and the beginnings of the present plant were erected on a 65-acre site (26.3 hectares) in the city's Sheffield Industrial Park. Several million dollars of expansion over

Robotic handling equipment transfers wheel discs through the various stages of manufacture.

the years have extended the manufacturing plant and administrative offices to 479,793 square feet (44,573 square meters).

Ownership of the London operations and others in the U.S. passed to Bain Capital in 1986 and the name was changed to Accuride. The overall Accuride operations were acquired in 1988 by Phelps Dodge Corporation of Phoenix, Arizona, and in 1997, they were purchased by the New York investment firm of Kohlberg Kravis Roberts & Co and members of Accuride management.

Over the past two years, Accuride Canada in London has introduced 20 new products, maintaining its leadership in the truck wheel production industry. Capital improvements at the plant have averaged about $6 million annually, including the increased use of robotic welding and materials handling, new technology and the use of automated systems.

Plant safety is a major program, and safety improvement is measuring a steady increase with attendant productivity improvements. Customer service is coordinated through a Customer Focused Manufacturing Council, which is directed by the senior management team. The plant sponsors major in-house training and development programs, which provide up to an average of 60 hours training per employee annually.

Accuride Canada supplies Ford, Navistar, Freightliner/Sterling, General Motors, Volvo, Mack Trucks, PACCAR(Kenworth/Peterbilt), Wabash National, Great Dane and Utility Trailer.

"We like to think that our long history as a leading London business, providing good jobs for Londoners and participating actively in the community, makes a beneficial contribution to the city," comments Doggett. "Thanks to the excellence of our products delivered by a highly trained workforce, we remain the major player in the truck wheel manufacturing industry."

Disc blanks are stamped out on this 2,000-ton press from steel coils weighing approximately 40,000 lbs.

GM DIESEL DIVISION

the technical needs of the company, creating job opportunities for its students.

As a major global exporter, GM Diesel Division has a well developed expertise in understanding and being competitively successful in world markets, an important ability for today's Canadian industries.

Diesel Division operations were established in 1950 to equip Canada's major railways with the new and highly efficient diesel-electric rail technology that replaced the era of steam. A half a century later the Division's continued use of new technology maintains the company as an innovative, worldwide leader in its two main markets.

Since the 1980s, DDGM has been the primary assembly operation for all General Motors' locomotive manufacturing, producing an average of 350 locomotives a year for railways in Canada, the United States and a total of 60 countries around the world. Up to 80 per cent of the diesel locomotives currently at work in Canada were produced in London.

In 1977 it established its Defence Operations and today is the world's number one builder of military light armoured vehicles (LAVs). The plant has built more than 3,500 such units in a wide variety of configurations for customers that include the United States Marine Corps, the Canadian Forces, the Australian Army, the Kingdom of Saudi Arabia and the United States National Guard. Diesel Division-built LAVs have seen military and peacekeeping duties in Cyprus, Panama, Somalia, Haiti, Bosnia, Kosovo and, in the hands of the U.S. Marines, in Operation Desert Storm during the Gulf War.

F rom listening to the wail of a diesel locomotive to watching television coverage of military forces on patrol, people hear and see products built by London's Diesel Division, General Motors of Canada Limited (DDGM) more often than they might imagine.

The DDGM plant, like the heavy locomotives and light armoured vehicles it turns out, dominates the landscape as the city's largest manufacturing industry with more than 2,700 employees and contractors. Hourly employees are members of Local 27, Canadian Auto Worker (CAW).

The plant plays a critical role in London's economy. Besides providing significant and important employment, GM Diesel Division offers jobs and training in the high-tech manufacturing sector, which is so vital in today's economy. Drawing its workforce from London and surrounding communities in southwestern Ontario, the plant has extensive on-the-job training programs to constantly upgrade skills, many of them highly specialized in welding and heavy metal fabrication. DDGM is also an important contributor to the nearby Fanshawe College where curriculums are matched with

LOCOMOTIVE OPERATIONS

The year 2000 marked the 50th anniversary for DDGM. Established in London to manufacture diesel-electric freight and passenger locomotives, the Division played a historic role in the transformation of the Canadian railway system from steam to diesel

power. Today, the Division continues to be a leading manufacturer of diesel-electric locomotives, and has delivered more than 7,600 units to customers in Canada and around the world.

DDGM London operations provide key manufacturing facilities for the GM Electro-Motive Division based in LaGrange, Illinois, and, since the late 1980s, has been the central assembly point for General Motors locomotives.

Over the years the plant has also been an important supplier of transit buses and school bus chassis. For a period beginning in 1965, the Division manufactured TEREX trucks and earthmoving equipment for major mining operations across Canada and

(above) The new and significantly bolder silhouette of the LAV III Armoured Personnel Carrier will soon support Canada's peacekeepers abroad.

(right) GM's new state-of-the-art 6,000-horsepower H-engine powers a new breed of heavy-hauling locomotive.

around the world. These mammoth vehicles utilized the same highly specialized diesel-electric technology already well developed for the Division's locomotive business.

When opened in 1950, the plant produced six types of locomotives ranging from 600 horsepower to 1,500 horsepower. Today the plant assembles state-of-the-art 4,000- to 6,000-horsepower heavy-hauling locomotives. The high-horsepower units utilize either AC or DC traction technologies that allow for maximum hauling efficiency. Today's high-horsepower locomotive moves as big a train as two units of the past, is more cost effective and operates with improved fuel efficiency.

The customer base for DDGM is unique, as there is a finite market for diesel locomotives of the size produced in London. In North America there are seven principal customers and while the plant supplies locomotives to many other countries, a significant customer-service and sales-support organization is required to build ongoing relationships and contracts. The Division sells directly to its customers, designing locomotives to meet specific needs of the railway. The company also maintains on-going contract maintenance agreements with many of its customers, providing technical and warranty support with GM specialists situated in the maintenance facilities of customers.

DEFENCE OPERATIONS

DDGM Defence Operations were established in 1977 with an initial order from the Canadian Forces for 491 light armoured vehicles. These high-speed, easily transported armoured vehicles have proven popular with armed forces around the world. More than 3,500 have been produced.

The plant produces a wide variety of light armoured vehicle configurations designed for specific military functions. They include troop deployment, ambulances for battlefield use, command and control vehicles with sophisticated communications equipment, rescue units for recovering disabled vehicles as well as front line combat and airfield defence units.

The London-produced LAVs are popular for peacekeeping duties with the Canadian armed forces where they are called upon for

(above) DDGM's new Flagship SD90MAC locomotive combines 6,000 horsepower with AC traction technology to deliver unprecedented levels of heavy-hauling performance.

(below) The most dramatic moment in the daily assembly process is when the fully assembled cab and long hood are lifted on to the waiting bogies.

reconnaissance work. New models are equipped with sophisticated surveillance and communication systems capable of detecting movement up to 10 kilometres away.

Along with the locomotive operations, the defence business unit provides contracts for more than 200 supplier companies across Canada, creating hundreds of spin-off jobs in all parts of the country.

"We're proud to be in London and provide good quality manufacturing job opportunities for Canadians," said Bill Pettipas, Executive Director, Diesel Division, General Motors of Canada Ltd. "For more than 50 years we have remained competitive because of the skills of our people."

"As a major Canadian exporting company, we accept that our success depends on our ability to understand the needs of our customers, to anticipate changes in those needs and to adapt quickly to change with the level of quality expected." ▐

JONES PACKAGING INC.

J ones Packaging Inc., with a family-owned business legacy of more than a century in London, today is a leading provider of packaging solutions for pharmaceutical and consumer product clients in Canada, the United States and Europe.

The company is widely recognized for its design expertise and quality of production in the pharmaceutical, health-care and confectionery packaging markets, a product focus it has maintained for much of its almost 120-year history. From its beginnings in the family home with a small press and cutter in the garage, Jones Packaging Inc. has prospered and grown to a large company, using today's state-of-the-art computerized process equipment in a new, modern London plant with a major subsidiary facility in nearby Guelph, Ontario.

Jones Packaging Inc. produces a wide array of products, including: folding cartons; prescription (dot matrix and dual web laser) and pressure-sensitive labels; shrink sleeves used for tamper-proof containers and full-body prime labels; custom-printed pharmacy bags; folded, flat and roll-fed inserts that contain directions and other mandatory information; vials; bottles; unit dose compliance packaging; and medication delivery systems. As well as being a major player in the pharmaceutical packaging field, the company is the leading supplier of a full range of prescription packaging needs to pharmacists and long-term health-care institutions across Canada and to a growing number of international customers.

(*above) Jones Packaging's roots: 1173 Dundas Street, 1932-1999.*

(*below left) New headquarters and manufacturing facility, 3000 Page Street. Opened 1999.*

"We're proud of our history in London as a family-owned company," says Chris Jones Harris, a fourth generation family member who, along with her husband Ron Harris, acquired control of the company in 1996. "The pharmacy and pharmaceutical markets are where our history has been and where we have had ongoing success. That market is growing, due particularly to the aging population in North America, and we see our future as continuing to be strong and competitive in what we do best."

It was in 1882 that Henry J. Jones, a compositor with the London Advertiser newspaper, and Frank Lawson, a news reporter with the paper, formed the Lawson and Jones Company, which specialized in general printing and specialty drug labels. By 1900 the firm was well known in the drug packaging field and employing 60 people. It was about the same time that the partners acquired a lithographic flatbed press, believed to be the first in the region. At the turn of the century, the rapidly growing company built its first plant on the east side of Clarence Street, on a site now occupied by the Galleria Mall.

Henry Jones took over the company upon the death of Frank Lawson in 1911 and in 1913 sold his interest to Ray Lawson, son of his former partner and a future Lieutenant Governor of Ontario. The name Lawson and Jones was retained while Henry Jones with his six sons established a new printing company, H. J. Jones-Sons Limited. The new Jones enterprise was a general printer of labels and catalogues and retained the drug-box and label business from the Lawson and Jones firm.

Following World War One, the three youngest Jones' sons, Floyd, Linton and Mervyn, (Chris' grandfather) established Jones Box and Label Limited to produce the drug labeling products. In 1932, construction was completed on a new building at 1173 Dundas Street for the growing firm. Sales of drug boxes and labels expanded over the next 15 years, and in 1944, the box making operations were moved to a branch factory in St. Thomas.

By 1951, a new addition to the Dundas Street plant doubled capacity and allowed the St. Thomas operations to move into the one London location. During the summer of 1952, Henry J. Jones, now in his 90th year, passed away leaving his three sons to continue operating the company.

In the subsequent 44 years, many members of the Jones family, including Chris's father, Bob, retained active senior leadership roles with the firm.

In the mid '70s, due to significant growth in the prescription packaging business, the marketing and distribution teams for this division moved to expanded space on Nightingale Avenue in the east end of London.

The company continued its strategic growth, and, in the early '80s, the web-printing division of Jones, which produces the labels, shrink sleeves and leaflets, outgrew its home on the fourth floor of 1173 Dundas Street, and a plant was acquired at the corner of Second Street and Oxford Street.

By the late '80s, serious capacity issues were being realized in the sheet-fed carton operations, which supported sales to the pharmaceutical, confectionery and consumer product markets. This situation was resolved through the acquisition, in 1988, of a folding carton company in Guelph, Ontario. The Guelph facility provided Jones with a state-of-the-art printing and distribution center and continues to support the substantial growth of the company.

1996 marked the beginning of a new era for the Jones company as Ron Harris and Chris Jones Harris acquired control and set out on an aggressive path of growth. With the new corporate name, Jones Packaging Inc., reflecting more accurately the business of the firm, the co-owners opened modern new premises at 3000 Page Street. The $15-million facility with state-of-the-art equipment launched Jones Packaging Inc. into the new century with dynamic plans for continued growth and expansion. The 132,000-square-foot London plant and the company's 128,000-square-foot facility in nearby Guelph have supported an increase in the workforce to 330 and allowed for its continued expansion into the global marketplace.

"Businesses with a long history of family ownership tend to attract and maintain loyal and committed employees, and that has certainly been our experience," says Ron Harris. "Almost half our workforce has been with Jones Packaging Inc. for more than 15 years and we have many employees who have been with us for all their working life. The jobs have changed over the years with many now requiring high levels of technical skills, and our team has grown with these changes."

The company takes particular pride in its ability to provide its customers with professional services from the initial design stage through

(above) Guelph, Ontario, manufacturing facility.

(below left) Partial view of manufacturing area of the Page Street location.

to the finished product. In-house graphic and structural specialists, using computer-aided design techniques, work directly with customers to bring added value to the packaging projects. Using internet-based communication technologies, company designers electronically provide customers with designs and services that formerly required outsourced graphics.

New presses, including an eight-station web flexo unit with in-line die-cutting capabilities and a six-colour litho press with an in-line, water-based coater, plus the latest in die-cutting and gluing equipment, provide leading-edge technology and contribute to the highest possible product quality.

Quality assurance management is a given for the company considering the bulk of its products are for the health-care and consumer-product industries. Barcode-based systems are used to control packaging integrity through inline electronic inspections and ensure the stringent demands and policies of its client base are strictly followed. In 1996, Jones Packaging Inc. became the first folding carton company in Canada to register to the ISO 9001 international standard series for quality management assurance.

Backed by a rich tradition dating back over the last century, Jones Packaging is clearly focused on what it needs to do to drive success into the next millenium.

"The shape of things to come may be uncertain to some, but Jones has what it takes to package the future." ◀

M^cCORMICK CANADA

McCormick Canada, the country's leading purveyor of spice, seasonings and flavouring products, has its head office and manufacturing facility for its retail and food service products at the 316 Rectory Street site.

M cCormick Canada is not only the country's leading purveyor of food spice, seasonings and flavouring products, but its London-based Club House division has historical links with the city going back to 1883. For well over a century, the company has been a major London employer and business leader.

Club House Foods Inc. had its beginnings in an old carpentry shop at the corner of Carling and Talbot Streets, in a company established by London businessmen W. J. Gorman and D. J. Dyson. Initial products were coffee, turpentine, liquid ammonia and sewing machine oil.

Spices and related baking products were added in 1885, under the Forest City brand. In 1886 R. C. Eckert joined the partnership and the company became known as Gorman, Eckert & Co. For the next 70 years, they were a leading London-based provider of spices, seasonings and specialty foods.

In the early years, spices were marketed to grocers in large, colourful containers, to be sold by the ounce in their stores. The housewife would fill her own containers at home. William Gorman, the initial company president, built his business policy around three words—honesty, integrity and quality. This philosophy served the company well, making the name "Club House" one of the most accepted trade names in Canadian kitchens.

From its beginning and continuing today, the London operations of McCormick have been marked by growth and expansion. After seven years

in a Clarence Street location, Gorman, Eckert & Co. had become the largest olive packing company in the British Empire and moved to its present site at 316 Rectory Street. The 1928 acquisition of another London company, IXL Spice and Coffee Mills, added peanut confections marketed under the Butternut label.

In 1939 William Gorman died. His family continued to manage company operations until 1959 when Gorman, Eckert & Co. was acquired by McCormick & Company of Baltimore, Maryland. McCormick & Company is the global leader in manufacturing, marketing and distribution of spices, seasonings and flavours to the food industry, including retail customers, foodservice and food processing businesses around the world.

A decade later, the Gorman, Eckert & Co. name was changed to Club House Foods Inc., reflecting the company's major Club House brand.

In 1960, the company began to market the McCormick line of gourmet spices in its distinctive green label glass jar. In 1965, seasonings and sauce mixes were added and as the company increased its emphasis on spices, seasonings and flavourings, products such as peanut butter and coffee were discontinued.

In 1989, Club House Foods Inc. merged with its sister companies Stange Canada and Food Ingredients, both located in Toronto, and the combined company was renamed McCormick Canada Inc. with its headquarters in London. The company has manufacturing, sales

The forward-looking philosophy evident in its product development is also apparent in the company's enlightened "Power of People" business philosophy in employee relations. In London, Club House employs approximately 480 people who are encouraged to participate at all levels in the progress and management of the company. Club House also supports the participation of its people in community activities and matches employee charitable donations for the good of the London community.

From humble London beginnings in a rented carpentry shop, McCormick's Club House division has grown to be the Canadian leader in its field, and enters the 21st Century as a proud and historic member of the city's business community. ◖

and distribution centres in Montreal, Toronto, Edmonton and Calgary. The Club House Division serves retail grocery and food service customers with a vast array of products such as spices, extracts, seasonings, salad dressings, sauces and gravy mixes, marinades, food colourings and cake decorating items.

The pattern set by William Gorman to anticipate changing customer needs through product development and diversification continues to be a strength of McCormick's Club House operations. Food tastes have become more exotic in recent years as Canadians seek out a wider variety of meals with new and bolder flavours. Consumption of spices has doubled in Canada during the past 10 years and Club House has successfully introduced a series of new flavourings under its "La Grille" and "One Step Seasonings" lines. In 1998, the company launched its Club House "a little means a lot" advertising campaign to support its many new products with television, print and outdoor media. A website, www.clubhouse-canada.com was added in 1999 to provide instant access for consumers.

The company recognizes that consumers desire more variety and new tastes, along with greater convenience in food preparation. Sales of value-added complex flavour products reflect the success of Club House in meeting customer expectations.

Since 1885, Club House spices and seasonings have played an integral role in Canadian kitchens. With Club House, a little means a lot.

LONDON HYDRO

London Hydro, like most other municipal electric utilities in Ontario, faces a new future with the new millennium.

In 2000, the provincial electricity industry began a process of deregulation whereby London Hydro changed from a city-owned utility to a market-focused, incorporated business. As it has for nearly 90 years, London Hydro will continue to provide safe, reliable electric power for London businesses, institutions and homes. It will maintain and expand its network of above and below ground distribution lines but, depending on the options selected for London, electric power customers will have competitive choices for the purchase of power.

London Hydro is the fifth largest electric utility in Ontario. During its long history, London Hydro has been recognized for its forward-thinking approach that has brought new technology to London homes and businesses and creating improvements in the way people live and work.

Early in the 20th Century, London and the introduction of affordable electric power were synonymous. Sir Adam Beck played a leading role in this achievement. This distinguished London businessman served simultaneously as London's mayor and member of the provincial legislature, but he is best known as the founder of the Hydro Electric Power Commission of Ontario in 1906. Under his direction, low-cost, publicly-generated electricity was made readily available throughout most of the province.

"Although some things are changing, what remains the same is our commitment to meeting the needs of our customers for a safe, clean, reliable supply of electricity at the lowest possible cost," says Bernie Watts, General Manager of London Hydro. "We have grown with London and we will continue to refine our system so as to maintain a high level of efficiency and our long tradition of excellence in all we do."

From its founding in November of 1910, London Hydro has been recognized as one of the better managed and more innovative

(above) London Hydro's Network Operations Centre.

electrical utilities in the province. Its retail division, which marketed the first electrical appliances to many London homes, today continues to supply the public with the latest in energy efficient appliances to help save time and money. London had the first underground serviced subdivision in postwar Canada and the program to place cables underground in place of overhead wires continues, a major factor in avoiding pruning of the many trees in the Forest City.

Today's London Hydro system is able to provide a peak load of 600 Megawatts through close to 2,000 kilometres of distribution lines spanning a territory of 410 square kilometres. Altogether, London Hydro provides energy products and services to more than 125,000 residential, institutional, industrial and business customers.

London Hydro's progressive approach continues through its launch of LONDONCONNECT, providing high-speed fibre connectivity through a metropolitan area network.

"Londoners have grown to expect London Hydro to be in the forefront with equipment, distribution networks, levels of service and the quality of our people," says Mr. Watts. "That's our legacy for the future." ▮▮

LONDONCONNECT

L ONDONCONNECT is the latest example of London Hydro's mission to continually add value to the services it provides to its customers.

LONDONCONNECT is a high-speed digital network that provides users with cutting edge technology not available through other systems. A data communications network made up of fibre optic cable and electronic routers, LONDONCONNECT offers secure and reliable virtual private networks to businesses, institutions and community organizations.

Users access the high-speed data connectivity through a Metropolitan Area Network (MAN) for their Internet and wide-area connections, allowing businesses to transform their office network into a community-wide area network. Customers are able to run all Internet Protocol applications including IP-video, IP-voice, NetMeeting and Tele-education.

"The program is the first of its kind to be offered by a Canadian utility and it illustrates the dynamic approach to business that London Hydro is working toward in a deregulated marketplace. It is truly a new era in business development for us," says Bernie Watts, General Manager of London Hydro. "In a global marketplace, we believe the London community needs a high-speed digital access to communicate internally and externally with the World Wide Web. As a community-based organization, London Hydro is now able to offer our valuable customers a new dimension in data communications providing them with a competitive advantage."

LONDONCONNECT's network is made up of fibre optic cable and electronic switches to create a fully redundant fail-safe high-speed community-wide network. With an infrastructure that consists of approximately 100 kilometres spanning across the city, LONDON-CONNECT offers high-speed connectivity at a fixed price rather than a usage time-dependent price. The community network also offers a level of service matched with the needs of the customer, giving users the connectivity scale required.

Both of London's major hospital complexes signed on early for LONDONCONNECT. St. Joseph's Health Care links Parkwood

Hospital and St. Joseph's Hospital with a private network allowing the two sites to operate electronically as one. London Health Sciences Centre uses LONDONCONNECT to obtain high-speed data and voice transfer at a reasonable cost. All London hospital internal telephones and pagers are routed over data networks, providing staff with direct access to any hospital site from any extension. Another valuable link supports videoconferences and medical imaging services. The secure, private network allows exchange of volumes of information including the transfer of patient files such as X-rays.

Other uses provide law firms the ability to search legal cases on remote databases, libraries to have high-speed Internet access and ability to search a wealth of worldwide databases and government customers a full suite of voice and data services.

"Fibre optics allow customers to transfer data 100 to 1,000 times faster than previously," says Mr. Watts. "LONDONCONNECT confirms our city's reputation as Canada's 'most connected city'." ◖

CARDINAL KITCHENS LIMITED

we've got the people and the technology in place to excel. That's what makes it work."

Mr. Lucy has what it takes to hold up his end of that bargain. He joined Cardinal in 1974 with an economics degree from the University of Western Ontario and four years of critically important business experience with IBM and Woods Gordon Management Consultants. He acquired the company in 1987.

As early as 1978, with Mr. Lucy as General Manager, the company converted its production line to a modular system using the European frameless cabinetry process with the high tech 32-mm concept. "We simplified production and cut our costs, something that is essential in a business that is both competitive and subject to the ups and downs of the home-building industry," said Mr. Lucy.

Beyond the technology and production techniques, however, the key to satisfying customers has been quality of design, finish and installation.

Mr. Lucy stresses that custom cabinetry is, essentially, a work of art. True to that spirit, Cardinal has focused attention—and investment—on the design and finishing of its cabinets. The company offers customers a computer-generated preview of design options as well as hand-done original perspective drawings for the more complex projects. Cardinal also pioneered the mixing of its own pigments for cabinet finishes; giving customers a choice of more than 2,200 finishes.

Cardinal's emphasis on quality has brought repeated awards from the London Home Builders Association for "the most outstanding kitchen" and, more recently, the same award at the provincial level, and has also allowed the firm to successfully add custom entertainment centers to its product line. ❧

F or nearly 40 years, Cardinal Kitchens has led the cabinetry industry in southwestern Ontario, by concentrating on two major goals—manufacturing and distributing the finest custom-made cabinetry in the country and designing specifically to its customers' imaginations.

Established in 1961 as a local builder and installer of kitchen cabinets and bathroom vanities, Cardinal Kitchens today is a leader not only in London and southwestern Ontario, but is also an aggressive competitor in the U.S. market. More than 30 per cent of the Exeter Road plant's production is destined for export, primarily in the prestigious Bloomfield Hills suburb of Detroit. The distinctive quality Cardinal cabinets can also be found in kitchens of homes in Australia, Florida, Bermuda, Portugal and South America.

Cardinal credits a high degree of its ongoing success to its ability to combine careful craftsmanship with state-of-the-art technology and sound management.

David M. Lucy, president and owner of Cardinal Kitchens, puts it this way: "I'm not a cabinet maker. I'm a businessman whose company happens to make cabinets, and as a businessman I've made sure I surround myself with good people.

"We have a relatively small staff of 48, but each employee is a professional in what he or she does. The average tenure of an employee is 18 years and that says to our customers that they are getting the best work from experienced craftsmen. My job is to know our markets, to understand what our customers want, and to make sure

Cardinal Kitchens Limited
Today, Tomorrow and for Years to Come
Website: www.cardinalkitchens.com

KAISER ALUMINUM & CHEMICAL OF CANADA LIMITED

K aiser Aluminum Engineered Products is an important and progressive part of the city's manufacturing sector, providing stable employment for skilled workers with the majority of its output exported to the United States. A wholly owned subsidiary and the only Canadian operation of the Kaiser Aluminum & Chemical Corporation, the London plant operates four shifts on a 24-hour-a-day schedule.

The London facility has two manufacturing processes. A newer function recycles aluminum and casts the melted material into aluminum logs and billets that are sold as raw material to numerous manufacturers. Customers include the truck-trailer industry, distributor (bar and rod), and a wide variety of manufacturing, marine, automotive and industrial applications.

A second function is an extrusion process where aluminum billets are pressed through dies to produce lengths of various standard and custom shapes. The plant is able to produce up to 65 million pounds of extrusions annually for customers in Canada and the U.S.

The company was moved to the new 255,000-square-foot plant in London after nearly 50 years in a smaller Scarborough facility. Plans call for a continued expansion into the automotive segment of the business, including blocks for automatic braking systems.

"The London operation has been highly productive and successful since it was established on our Gore Road site in 1992," said Theordore J. DiGuiseppe, group vice president of Kaiser. "Our growth and the continued quality of our production demonstrate that the move to London was a very good move for both Kaiser and London."

The excellence of the company was recognized in 1998 with the London Chamber of Commerce Outstanding Business Achievement Award. This award, made by a Chamber judging panel, gave the plant top marks among city companies for its management, staff relations, competitiveness, productivity and community contribution.

(above) The London site, Kaiser Aluminum and Chemical Corporation's only Canadian operation, has been highly productive since its move to the 255,000-square-foot plant on Gore Road. Kaiser Aluminum believes in the pursuit of excellence as shown through its highly skilled and team-focused workforce, its satisfied customers and its adherance to strictly regulated quality standards.

(below) Preparation of molten aluminum for casting of extrusion billets.

Pursuit of excellence has been a theme of the company since it was established. In 1996 Kaiser become ISO 9002 certified and in 1998 achieved its QS9000 certification. The company is regularly recognized for product design and by its customers as a preferred supplier.

Mr. DiGuiseppe pays tribute to the quality of the plant's workforce. The company encourages training and upgrading of skills by its workers and assists in program costs for approved education.

"At Kaiser Aluminum we continue to explore new paths, products, processes, expanding capital efforts, discovering new technologies and, hopefully, creating lasting value for our owners. Whether it's a problem to be solved, an opportunity to be explored, a key business to be re-engineered, or a product or technology to be developed, we focus on change and learning, for both our customers and ourselves."

Kaiser believes that creating value for its customers requires the London company to not only survive but thrive and grow, being able to adapt to change swiftly, systematically and continuously. Not just learning to manage a one-time improvement effort, but learning to see all of its efforts as improvements.

Kaiser reaches its goals by learning to learn. ❙❚

R H O - C A N

Rho-Can Machine and Tool Company Ltd. is a dynamic Canadian and London story of entrepreneurial success.

Established in 1984 by brothers Alf and Cas Marques and D. de Jesus, the company is a significant tier-two supplier to the automotive industry, specializing in total service from engineering, tools and dies, and jigs and fixtures, to general machining and custom parts and special purpose machines. Its workforce of 80 includes professionally skilled designers, toolmakers, welders, machinists, millwrights and fabricators, most recruited and trained by Rho-Can.

"We're kind of unique in that we are involved from start to finish for our customers," says Mr. de Jesus, sales manager of the company. "Unlike some companies that specialize in tools and dies, we provide a full line of products and services. That assures our customers we are able to meet their specific requirements and that we are able to follow through with products they need. This has made Rho-Can a very attractive partner as manufacturers have looked to outsourcing."

The three owners were trained in the tool and die profession in the former Rhodesia in Africa, thus the name Rho-Can. Canada offered immigration opportunities, and government authorities recommended London because of its relative size and location. An initial plant was established in Lambeth, and in 1994, the steadily expanding company was relocated to its modern 31,000-square-foot facility on Industrial Road. Most of its customers are in the south-western Ontario auto industry but the company also does business international-ly, including in Mexico.

The company prides itself on a tradition of superior quality and services

at all levels of its technical resources and production facilities, and has completed ISO 9001 certification. The owners say a constant challenge is to attract, train and retain highly skilled tradesmen, which make up the core value of Rho-Can, and the company does most of its own training in cooperation with Ontario's community colleges and training institutions.

"Ours is a business where close tolerance product quality, on-time delivery and personalized customer service count," says Alf Marques, who manages cost estimating and planning for Rho-Can. "This means we use the latest computer technology and remain constantly up-to-date on product evolution. Our customers expect us to live and breathe quality every day, and we do that."

Rho-Can is also proud of its ongoing contributions to the community through the provision of skilled jobs, sponsorship of athletic teams and as a strong and growing industrial company.

Rho-Can—People, technology and engineering excellence for the 21st Century. ◼

(above left) Unlike some automotive suppliers, Rho-Can specializes in total service, using the latest computer technology to provide a full line of up-to-date products and services.

(below) Rho-Can's modern 31,000-square-foot facility on Industrial Road is home to a workforce of 80 professionally skilled designers, toolmakers, welders, machinists, millwrights and fabricators, most recruited and trained by Rho-Can.

C H A P T E R

12

T W E L V E

Technology and
Communications

Photo by Mike Grandmaison

MICROTRONIX SYSTEMS LTD.

combination of electrical instruments, acoustic test fixtures and a fully programmable microcomputer made it exactly what was needed by the manufacturers of the day and led to the rapid growth of Microtronix. Within a short period of time Microtronix had expanded into the United States, United Kingdom, Germany and the Far East. To date Microtronix equipment is sold in over 35 countries worldwide.

WORLDWIDE REPRESENTATION

Supporting the sale of specialized technology products to the global market place is no mean feat and Microtronix does not do it alone. Microtronix products are supported by a large group of representatives located strategically around the world so that customers have access to knowledgeable sales and technical people almost anywhere. Technical and sales representatives routinely attend in-depth training programs at Microtronix to stay up to date with latest developments.

CORPORATE PHILOSOPHY

A fundamental part of the company philosophy and a reason for its continued success is the adherence to recommended testing

I ncorporated in 1972, Microtronix Systems Ltd. provides innovative electronic solutions to unique problems for industries in North America and around the world. Located in a 3,700-square-metre facility in London, Ontario, Canada, Microtronix designs and builds special purpose test equipment for the telephone industry worldwide. From the very early years and up to the present Microtronix has quietly contributed to the success of giants like AT&T, Nortel, Lucent, Siemens and many more. When fast production test solutions are needed it is Microtronix that provides the answers.

EARLY COMPANY HISTORY

In the early years the company designed and manufactured custom telephone testing equipment for the local Northern Telecom plant, but in the years between 1975 and 1985 the company set off in a new direction. Rather than just making custom products for a specific customer, Microtronix developed its own products that could be sold to the general market.

The deregulation of the telephone market in North America in the early 1980s presented a new opportunity. Telephone manufacturers wishing to sell in North America would now be required to test their phones to meet national standards. A method to accurately and rapidly test telephones was required. It was in this climate that the Model 60 Telephone Test Set was born. This unique and innovative

(right) Telephone acoustic testing is one area where Microtronix is a world leader in providing extremely accurate and cost-effective solutions.

standards where they already exist. The Microtronix Research and Development department takes this information and designs equipment to provide test methods and results based on the sound research and recommendations of globally recognized standards bodies. Using this approach means that Microtronix measurements can be correlated with the laboratory. Microtronix staff contribute directly to the Telephone Industry Association (TIA) standards committee and are recognized for their broad experience and dedication to accuracy.

A major difference between Microtronix test equipment and other test equipment makers is that Microtronix is focused on the task of providing solutions for telephone manufacturing rather than the laboratory. Usually this means learning the real needs of the industry

(above) Customers and representatives from around the world regularly take advantage of training courses conducted at the Microtronix facility in London, Canada.

and mixing hardware and software into a product that addresses the needs of the test engineer rather than the scientist. In some cases however, the ease of use, fast testing time and accuracy of the Microtronix equipment has meant that laboratories use Microtronix as an adjunct to other equipment.

THE FUTURE

As the 21st century begins Microtronix is extending its special expertise to the next communication revolution—the cellular telephone. A highlight of the Microtronix product line has been the ability to provide very accurate measurements of the acoustic qualities of a telephone. In the early years of cell phones it seemed that sound quality took a back seat to simply making the telephone work. Now as the cell phone matures the industry is under pressure to provide clear connections of the type we commonly experience with conventional telephones. Microtronix has adapted their acoustic expertise to allow cell phone makers to make these same acoustic evaluations on cellular telephones. This new venture has great potential and is only the beginning of new products that will continue to bring the technology of Microtronix Systems to the world. ◗

THE JOHN P. ROBARTS RESEARCH INSTITUTE

The John P. Robarts Research Institute is a Canadian success story with an international reputation for excellence in medical research since its establishment in 1986 as Canada's only privately operated and directed medical research centre. In a few short years, the Institute has realized an impressive list of major discoveries, won prestigious awards and made vital contributions to medical science and technology commercialization.

Centre, has steadily expanded its research capabilities in step with its increased sources of funding. Today, the Institute is one of the city's largest employers with well over 400 scientists, research associates, technicians, trainees and support personnel. Its state-of-the-art facility adjacent to the University Campus of LHSC, is made up of 90,000 square feet of laboratory space. Special features include a transgenic mouse facility, a DNA sequencing facility, a FACs core facility, laser-guided confocal imaging suite, a 4-Tesla functional Magnetic Resonance Imaging suite, a 3D Computed Rotational Angiography suite and a number of other unique imaging modalities.

More than 30 patentable medical discoveries have been made at Robarts, and the Institute has begun to spin off private companies to commercialize on its discoveries to earn revenues for reinvestment in research. This competitive and entrepreneurial approach by Robarts clearly illustrates the Institute's growing reputation for efficiency, excellence and leadership in support of improved health and better medicine. ⁋

"Organizations are frequently asked to articulate a vision," says Dr. Mark Poznansky, President and Scientific Director. "Ours is simple—we want to make a difference—to make substantial contributions to medical research in the belief that it will save lives, save health care dollars and create jobs. We choose to not only be a leading medical research institute, but in fact, we want to play an essential role in the 'New Economy'."

The Robarts Research Institute, its Board, scientists and staff believe the Institute is part of the leading edge of change in the Canadian economy as it shifts its focus to knowledge-based industries in the areas of biology, medicine, biotechnology, pharmaceuticals and medical devices. After several years of growth and expansion, The John P. Robarts Research Institute is well positioned in the areas of diabetes and other autoimmune diseases, transplantation, stroke and neurodegenerative diseases, vascular disease, gene therapy and molecular virology, advanced imaging, clinical trials, and clinical pharmacology.

"We are encouraged that our two senior levels of government have a clear commitment to the country's economic development through knowledge-based industries in which the Institute plays such an essential role in support of our health care system," continues Dr. Poznansky. "We will continue to support this environment of creativity and discovery, which we know will make a difference to the health of all Canadians and job and wealth creation. We are creating value through research."

The John P. Robarts Research Institute, affiliated with The University of Western Ontario and London Health Sciences

(above left) The John P. Robarts Research Institute.

(below) The 4-Tesla functional Magnetic Resonance Imaging suite has the highest magnetic field of any human scanner in Canada. Using radio waves and magnetic fields, fMRI can produce images of the working brain. Pictured from left, Dr. David Holdsworth and Dr. Ravi Menon.

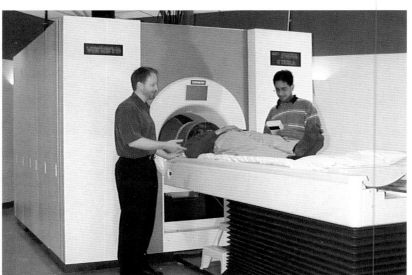

THE LONDON BIOTECHNOLOGY INCUBATOR

Artistic rendition of the proposed biotechnology commercialization center prepared by G & G Partnership Architects, 2000.

E stablishment of The London Biotechnology Incubator in The University of Western Ontario Research Park is a key step for London into the exciting, worldwide growth industry of biotechnology.

London's biotechnology commercialization centre will contribute directly to economic growth and job creation by providing state-of-the-art physical space, and an array of business and technical support to entrepreneurs. While having a primary focus on biotechnology, the incubator will be receptive to all related engines of economic growth, and all related disciplines which can benefit from such a facility, including medicine, engineering and computer science.

The biotechnology industry across North America has experienced significant growth since 1985, expanding from a market capitalization of $50 million to over $120 billion in 1998, and employing more than 150,000 people. The sector is poised for significant growth in Canada, as has been shown by the significant emphasis and interest being shown by both the public and private sectors.

In the London area, approximately 2,000 people are employed full-time in an academic medical research setting, and 8 to 10 biotechnology/medical device companies are currently London-based. As part of the development of a strategic plan for growth and retention of new and emerging businesses in the area, it was determined that London has significant potential to develop a commercialization centre for biotechnologies—in the areas of human health, environmental and agricultural sciences, as well as for broader technologies originating from within both academic institutions and the private sector.

The main goal of the incubator will be to produce successful firms that will leave the facility financially viable and free standing, remain in the community and contribute to further economic development. By providing emerging biotech companies with desirable space, access to science, services and their target workforce, London will build a critical mass and a global biotechnology presence.

The origins of The London Biotechnology Incubator were in June 1999 when local biomedical research and academic institutions, having been successful in spinning off biotechnology enterprises, resolved to establish a biotechnology commercialization center in London to serve as the southwestern Ontario hub for biotechnology commercialization activity. The founding shareholders were The John P. Robarts Research Institute, London Health Sciences Centre Research Corporation, Lawson Research Institute, The University of Western Ontario and the City of London. Together with regional private-sector and public-sector partners and the Province of Ontario, LBI successfully raised over $10 million to construct and operate The London Biotechnology Incubator.

LBI has sought and received support from The London Chamber of Commerce, London Economic Development Corporation, the Richard Ivey School of Business and various interested private sector individuals—both investors and potential tenants. Through discussions with the University of Guelph, the Ontario Ministry of Agriculture and Foods (OMAFRA) and Agriculture Ontario, LBI achieved an important regional focus.

There is every reason to believe that biotechnology will constitute a major driving force for job and wealth creation, and the establishment of The London Biotechnology Incubator makes the city a strong contender to be a major participant and helps London benefit from that economic growth. ◖

O E S , I N C .

I f innovation alone makes a company unique, OES, Inc. qualifies hands down. Since its inception in 1979, the company's growth has largely been based on its ability to successfully provide electronic solutions to previously unfulfilled control problems.

Now 40 employees strong and based in a new facility, OES's critical software and hardware technologies are fully developed in-house by a talented design team comprising engineers, technicians and technologists from many disciplines including electronics, electrical, civil and mechanical engineering and computer science fields.

A diverse and loyal customer base has resulted from production of practical, well-suited and user-friendly control devices and/or systems for a wide variety of applications. OES has responded by investing in skilled, talented and energetic people, and by furnishing the facilities, equipment and training needed to succeed in a solution-oriented company.

OES's focus on providing innovative control-product solutions has led to the achievement of many world "firsts" and patents. These have been possible through a commitment to continuous research and development. OES dedicates 25 per cent of its resources to research and development, whereby methods and technologies for all new products are investigated, offering its customers the newest available technology.

Not only does OES provide innovative answers, it steadfastly believes that customer service is imperative. The company's policies and procedures are founded on the principle that a product is not complete, a job is not a success, until the customer is satisfied. Service and support are built into OES's products, determined at the design stages and continued into the field.

OES is proud of the diversity of its products. Quality-assurance devices for the automotive wire harness industry, user interfaces for wastewater disinfection systems, recreational scoreboards, industrial signboards, controllers for industrial band saws and agricultural batchers are only a sampling of the products OES is capable of producing. Systems for snowmaking, log processing, fertilizer blending, lighting management, and "Dutch Clock" auctions have been designed and developed. The company believes that the list of future products will be limited only by need and imagination.

Innovation is further enhanced by a commitment to excellence for both products and people. ISO 9001 has proven to be an effective tool to achieve quality goals. Teamwork and accountability, exceeding expected standards, striving for excellence and continuous improvement are but some of the practices OES employs in its day-to-day operations.

High-tech research and development is performed in OES's lab.

Employees are encouraged to bring their best efforts to the workplace, and the company supports the upgrading of skills in time and funding. Suggestions for improvements are welcomed and seriously considered. Employees are also given opportunity to grow within the company, as illustrated by the many people who have taken on a management role.

Much of OES's success has been through effective working collaborations with recognized international industry leaders in various high-tech fields. OES has formed lasting partnerships by designing products that can be integrated into a variety of applications. Recent spin-offs of application-specific companies for snowmaking control ("IST"), automotive quality assurance (OES-A) and internet auctions (OES-Auction) have expanded business potential.

The future of technology is exciting and OES looks forward to applying innovative approaches to future challenges and opportunities. ▮

B I O N I C H E
L I F E   S C I E N C E S   I N C .

The dramatic global growth of biotechnology research and development companies was heralded in London as early as 1979 with the establishment of Vetrepharm, the founding company of Bioniche Life Sciences Inc.

Today, Bioniche Life Sciences is a fully integrated, Canadian biopharmaceutical company engaged in research, development, production and commercialization of proprietary technologies and products for international human and animal health markets. The Company, led by Graeme McRae, President and CEO, has three operating units: Bioniche Therapeutics, the human health division; Vetrepharm, the animal health unit; and Bioniche Pharma, which develops, manufactures and distributes sterile injectables and other pharmaceutical products. Founded and expanded in London, Bioniche is now poised to be a major Canadian player in both animal and human health markets as a result of its successful research and development program in cancer treatment and immunotherapy.

Vetrepharm Animal Health was established by Graeme McRae more than 20 years ago to engage in the research, development and marketing of animal health products. "We formed Vetrepharm because I was convinced major companies in the veterinary field were not placing serious research emphasis on the immune response and its interaction with animal disease, something that we hear a lot more about today," says Mr. McRae. Vetrepharm is now the largest Canadian-owned animal health biopharmaceutical company, with production facilities in London and Atlanta, Georgia, and marketing subsidiaries in Canada, the U.S., Australia and Europe, with exports to Latin America and the Middle East as well. Folltropin, Vetrepharm's lead product, is the world leader in FSH, a follicle-stimulating hormone for embryo transfer in cattle.

By 1990, it was apparent that the veterinary technologies could be successfully applied to human medicine. "We created Bioniche to research and ultimately commercialize the Vetrepharm technologies in human health," added Mr. McRae. "Our progress has been significant and we're pleased today to be a major Canadian player in the rapidly developing, worldwide biotechnology industry." The company has been very successful in marketing two proprietary products internationally, Suplasyn®, a treatment for Osteoarthritis and Cystistat®, for the treatment of Interstitial Cystitis, a painful, debilitating bladder condition.

The Bioniche Therapeutics division conducts pre-clinical research within the Biotechnology Research Institute of the National Research Council in Montreal. Therapeutics is responsible for scientific discovery, in-vitro and in-vivo pre-clinical research and development of human health products derived from proprietary technologies. The development of patented mycobacterial cell wall-DNA complex (MCC) formulations as a potential treatment for

(above) London Corporate Offices.

(below) Graeme McRae, founder of Vetrepharm and president and CEO of Bioniche Life Sciences.

bladder and prostate cancers is one of the key components of its research program and is expected to be the foundation for significant future growth for the company.

Bioniche Pharma operates a facility in Galway, Ireland, for the development, manufacture and distribution of sterile injectable pharmaceuticals in vials, ampoules and pre-filled syringes to a growing, multi-billion-dollar market.

In September 1999, Bioniche acquired a 137,000-square-foot pharmaceutical-manufacturing plant in Belleville, Ontario. This new facility will feature state-of-the-art animal health research laboratories and a large manufacturing operation to allow Bioniche to meet increasing worldwide demand for its veterinary products as well as for the company's proprietary formulations in development for cancer.

"Bioniche is well positioned in international markets. Our corporate drug discovery and development program ensures we will remain on the leading edge of the biotech sector," says Graeme McRae. "Biotechnology is a rapidly expanding global industry and, as a Canadian company founded here in London, we're proud to be one of the leaders." ▮

Business, Finance and the Professions

CITY OF LONDON

London's historic downtown is in good hands, thanks to the recent introduction of Canada's first Main Street program which uses a proven model to draw on local volunteer expertise for its creative marketing and promotional efforts. Two other agencies—Tourism London and London Economic Development Corporation—are also providing additional opportunities for the private sector to be a more active partner in attracting business investment to create additional jobs and grow the city's population.

The Forest City takes a systematic and planned approach to meeting the needs of its citizens, conscious at all times to maintain reasonable levels of municipal taxation through careful budgeting and controlled spending. City Council has served notice of its firm intention to hold the line on taxation and costs to its citizens—as evidenced in the City's ongoing success at keeping borrowing costs down, thanks to the renewal of its AAA credit rating.

While carefully positioning its major economic pieces to emphasize that London is customer driven and business friendly, the City is also giving priority to improving the quality of municipal services and facilities. In recent years, for instance, London nearly doubled its number of indoor swimming opportunities with the opening of two new pool complexes in the City's heavily populated east and south neighbourhoods. Ongoing improvements in the Thames Valley Parkway have been realized through the expansion of multi-use pathways and construction of pedestrian footbridges to encourage physical recreation and healthier forms of commuting. A nine-hole golf course, designed especially to accommodate the needs of the disabled, was also opened—the first of its kind in Canada.

Through the revitalization of its downtown and historic East London, the upgrading of recreational facilities and supporting significant capital works to encourage future development, City Council is committed to "Investing in the Community." A major tourism attraction is the Canada Summer Games to be held in August 2001 when many thousands of athletes and visitors will use the City's sports facilities, including a new 8000-seat multi-use stadium at the renowned University of Western Ontario and an expanded London Aquatic Centre.

The City of London moves forward into the 21st century with a renewed spirit of optimism and clear strategies for building a strong, vibrant London economy for the benefit of all Londoners.

City Council is firmly committed to fulfilling two broad goals of working to create an economic environment that encourages job creation, and ensuring that London remains a safe, clean and healthy functioning community. The pursuit of these goals, already under way, will guide the direction of *London—The Forest City*.

The City's agenda is both challenging and comprehensive, but ultimately achievable, through City Council initiated programs combined with the efforts of significant private enterprises and the major contribution of the community's large public sector organizations.

London is recognized as a major economic centre with a special focus on medical care and education. Its progress is ensured by a community spirit that cherishes volunteerism, encourages the sharing of innovative ideas and fosters activities that create local pride. Care is taken to provide opportunities for all citizens to actively participate in major decisions that affect their future.

(above) Local Pride. London—the Forest City.

(right) The development of a new downtown market is a key component in the revitalization of the city's core. The recently opened Covent Garden Market is a jewel in the crown of London's downtown.

City Council's Downtown Millennium Plan Committee recommendations are restoring confidence for the future of the City's core. A jewel in the downtown crown is the newly constructed Covent Garden Market, which by its design spawns memories of previous market buildings on this historic site. The downtown presence will be further strengthened with plans for the addition of a multi-purpose entertainment/arena facility to be built by a private sector partnership.

The future vision for London's core also calls for continuing beautification near the Forks of the Thames, the original beginning of London. An eye-catching addition will be the installation of a river fountain with clusters of water jets highlighted by multi-coloured lighting and music. Existing riverside parks and riverbank walkways draw many thousands of visitors and London residents to the pleasant ambiance of the Thames River.

London's Convention Centre continues to draw increasing business to the city by hosting such notable events as the national Reform Party Convention along with other significant conferences held by the Ontario Medical Association, the Federation of Canadian Municipalities and the Canadian Society for Civic Engineering Conference, to name but a few.

The City also took an active part in the privatization of the London airport and the establishment of The Greater London International Airport Authority. Plans are in the works to capitalize on the airport, with a new Industrial Park, major railway facilities and London's unique location on the 401/402 NAFTA Superhighway links to stimulate the future economy.

A concentrated program to rebuild and expand London's streets, sewage treatment plants and other necessary parts of the infrastructure continue apace in recognition that renewal is necessary to ensure adequate, reliable facilities and to allow for future growth.

London is indeed open for business. The recommendations of City Council's Small Business Task Force have very quickly transformed City departments and employees from "rule enforcers" to "problem solvers." This new customer service stance of City Hall is paying significant

(above) London's Thames Valley Parkway—home to many summer festivals and recreational activities.

dividends by shortening plan and permit approvals. Coupled with the improved access to the City's redesigned interactive website, these changes make doing business in London faster and more convenient.

It's all part of the City's strategy to move aggressively into the new century with a renewed vision for future development and a re-dedication toward preservation of an admirable community. ◗

(left) The City of London is a major partner in the 2001 Canada Summer Games. As a part of the community project, the University of Western Ontario is building an 8,000-seat multi-use stadium.

E S A M   G R O U P

The names "Cherryhill" and "Sam Katz" are instantly recognizable in London. They identify the city's best known community for senior citizens and the man responsible for the realization of a personal dream.

Situated just off Oxford Street West, the Cherryhill complex of 13 high-rise apartment buildings houses more than 2,800, the majority of them seniors, but also with tenants from all ages including students and professional couples. The units are grouped behind Cherryhill Village Mall, a mecca not only for the nearby residents, but also for seniors across the city who are attracted to the ambiance of a community with their interests at heart.

Harvey Katz, who with his brother, Howard, operates Esam Group, which runs the complex, says today's unique seniors' community wasn't the original plan of their father Sam. "It just happened that way, and we're all the better for it."

with Ewald Bierbaum. After building a number of homes elsewhere in the city, the partners acquired 50 acres of what could best be described as swampland in the former London Township and drained it as the site of the future Cherryhill development.

The original Westown Plaza, now Cherryhill Village Mall, opened in 1960 and construction began on the first of the high-rise apartment buildings.

"The apartment buildings were not built to attract any particular age group," says Harvey Katz. "In the beginning we had a majority of singles and university students as tenants but as they moved on the seniors moved in—and stayed. Today about 80 per cent are seniors, and we have a waiting list of retirees who want to be a part of this community. At the same time, Londoners of all ages are attracted to be residents in our rather unique setting."

Harvey and Howard carry on for their father who is disabled by several strokes.

The tragedies and family disruptions of World War Two in Europe shaped the dream of Sam Katz. Forced with his family from their home in the former Czechoslovakia, he emerged from five years in a Hungarian labour camp to find he and a sister were all that was left of their family. He immigrated to Canada in 1949 and a few years later in London formed the Esam development company

"He had a simple philosophy that said we each have a responsibility to help other people," they say. "There is no doubt that the hardships of his early years contributed to his determination to make life better for others. Perhaps having experienced communities and families torn apart led him to focus on making a happy home where people could be content and enjoy time with friends, particularly in their older years. We think that's a wonderful way of looking at life and we continue with it."

Perhaps nothing illustrates the attractive amenities and pace of life at Cherryhill better than the nearby garden plots provided by Esam for the use and enjoyment of tenants. Many senior tenants who left their home gardens when they retired and moved to Cherryhill, enjoy not only the opportunity to continue their hobby but also the friendships gained from working their plots alongside others.

The Cherryhill Village Mall is the focal point for the community. With 50 stores including a large food market, the Mall is the official gathering place for both residents and seniors from elsewhere in the city.

(top) Sam Katz, founder of the Esam Group.

(left) Situated just off Oxford Street West, the Cherryhill complex of 13 high-rise apartment buildings houses more than 2,800, the majority of them seniors.

The stores cater to the needs of seniors, offering preferred items and special services such as the public library branch which stocks more than the usual numbers of large print books. The mall concourse has a generous supply of benches so that strollers and shoppers can rest and chat while watching the passing crowds. The food court is a constant centre of activity where friends meet for coffee or a snack, and where a TV monitor highlights upcoming events of interest. Entertainment with music geared to seniors is a regular feature.

The Mall is also home to the Cherryhill Activity Club, which sees residents play cards, pool and darts, and where the overall sense of community is extended. Nearby is the newly expanded, 52-lane Fleetway Bowling Centre, also owned by Esam, providing both five- and ten-pin bowling enjoyment. The Centre, a popular recreational and gathering site for families of all ages, is both non-smoking and alcohol-free.

"We've made many changes to the Mall over the years with a view to giving it the look and feel of an old-time town square," says Harvey Katz. "The storefronts create the ambiance of a village and it's clear the Cherryhill residents feel a strong sense of belonging both in the Mall and throughout the complex. That's all in line with what Dad saw for Cherryhill—a comfortable place that is safe and easily accessible, where you can be with friends."

The special experience of community generated at Cherryhill is regularly cited by urban planning specialists as relatively unique, not only for London, but probably in North America. Its development as a desirable destination for seniors to live and congregate is seen as the direct result of the dream and the work of Sam Katz. His sons agree. "He made it easy for us to continue the success of Cherryhill. If at any time we ponder a decision about the future, all we have to do is remember his gentle reminder to 'take care of people'." ◄

(above right) The Cherryhill Village Mall is the focal point for the community. With 50 stores including a large food market, the Mall is the official gathering place for both residents and seniors from elsewhere in the city.

(right) Perhaps nothing illustrates the attractive amenities and pace of life at Cherryhill better than the nearby garden plots provided by Esam for the use and enjoyment of tenants. Photo by The London Free Press.

THE LONDON CHAMBER OF COMMERCE

political and economic policies that improve the city's economy and its quality of life.

Key issues include: education, taxation, transportation, infrastructure, research and development, economic development, health care and government reform. The Chamber remains London's only city-wide, completely independent business organization. Governed by a volunteer Board of Directors and managed by a dedicated administrative staff, its experience and history have enabled it to fight for vital issues over both the long and short term.

Just because the Chamber looks at the big picture doesn't mean that it forgets about the day to day challenges faced by London businesses and entrepreneurs. It offers an extensive range of services to ensure that whether members are interested in business development or government reform, their needs are met. Social events, training seminars, employee benefits insurance, political forums, Business After Five trade shows, networking breakfasts, Corporate Challenge and the annual gala Business Achievement Awards are all key services providing members with opportunities to build their business—and to get the most out of their membership.

While the Chamber's traditional role as an advocate for London business remains central, the organization has also responded to changing times with new approaches. Advances in technology have made it easier to keep members in touch with Chamber activities, allowing volunteers to be recruited on a project by project basis. That, in turn, allows members to define the terms on which they become involved rather than being forced to make an "all or nothing" choice between involvement and apathy. The advent of the World Wide Web, fax and e-mail communications have also made it possible to respond quickly to opportunities for high-profile guest speakers and presenters, enabling such events to be executed within days, rather than in weeks or months as in years past.

Changing times have also brought an increased focus on providing members with information valuable to their business, whether through member communications, or seminars and guest speaker events.

T he London Chamber of Commerce today continues a proud history of serving the interests of its members and the community, stretching over nearly 150 years.

The commitment of the London Chamber of Commerce is as strong now as when the first 40 members founded it in 1857. So is the Chamber's vision of a community where the private sector is the driving force in the economy, where governments work in partnership with business to improve the quality of life, and where public and private sectors share the same goals for a clean, safe and healthy community, while striving to improve its global competitiveness.

The Chamber's many achievements flow from its mission to serve as the voice of London's business community. Through a well-developed network, members volunteer their expertise, opinions and enthusiasm to the organization, which in turn uses those resources to promote social,

(above) The "Boardroom" of the London Chamber of Commerce plays host to the Board of Directors and many of the committees that comprise the Chamber's Policy, Program and Communication's portfolios. The Boardroom can be rented out, but to members only.

(right) Networking is the name of the game for many of the Chamber's 1,500 plus members. Photo by Ted Smith, Wonderland Graphics.

If knowledge is power, the Chamber's goal is to make certain that its members are some of the most powerful business people around.

Similarly, advocacy efforts have been enhanced to better reflect changes to London's economic landscape. The Chamber was an early supporter of efforts to promote London as a centre for biotechnology. It was a partner in founding London's Economic Development Corporation. And it has worked with the public sector to support increased investment in London's health-care infrastructure. Internally, the Chamber has founded an Export Club to better reflect the importance of international sales to the city's future economic growth. And it has added groups focusing on such important growth areas as information technology and e-commerce.

The Chamber is an active participant in community building. Volunteers and senior administration work regularly with local trade and industry groups and have forged ongoing partnerships with London's health-care and education sectors. Several of its major annual events incorporate charity fundraising. And while the Chamber isn't afraid to speak out to government on behalf of business, it also works with government—particularly local government—in the interests of the community.

The last 143 years have shown the London Chamber of Commerce consistently representing the voice of business—because business is its heart, and its strength. The next 143 years will be equally dedicated to the same principles of leadership. ◗◗

(above) The Chamber of Commerce building at 244 Pall Mall Street is centrally located directly behind the Station Park Inn and facing Richmond Row. It is the centre of all activity for the the hundreds of Chamber volunteers who refer to it as the home of London's "Voice of Business." Photo by M. Grandmaison.

(below) London's skyline resembles many of Canada's larger cities, yet London retains the convenience and ambiance of a smaller community. Many people come to London for business and end up staying for life. Photo by M. Grandmaison.

ERNST & YOUNG

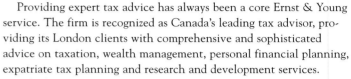

Ernst & Young has been a leading member of the London area business community for more than 50 years, providing high-quality business advice to a broad spectrum of industries ranging from up-and-coming entrepreneurs to Canada's largest multinational companies. Situated in One London Place, the team of dedicated professionals offers outstanding expertise to assist clients in managing their growth.

The London Ernst & Young team draws from its North American network and global presence to provide local, personalized client service. As part of a dynamic, worldwide organization, Ernst & Young in London provides assurance and advisory business services and consulting in areas as diverse as acquisitions, divestitures, financing, corporate recovery and insolvency services, strategic planning and e-commerce.

Providing expert tax advice has always been a core Ernst & Young service. The firm is recognized as Canada's leading tax advisor, providing its London clients with comprehensive and sophisticated advice on taxation, wealth management, personal financial planning, expatriate tax planning and research and development services.

Whether a company is in start-up or expansion mode, growth poses special challenges, often stretching its people, systems and financing. Using a team approach, Ernst & Young specialists assist companies to successfully develop business opportunities and to create value for shareholders.

For companies poised to enter new markets, Ernst & Young offers extensive support concerning all aspects of business environments, market surveys and feasibility studies, introduction of potential business partners, advice on corporate structures, and joint ventures and e-commerce.

The London operations were begun as Clarkson Gordon in 1948 led by Ken Lemon with eight staff members. The name changed in 1989 when Clarkson Gordon became a member of Ernst & Young.

"Over the years, we have grown with London and with our clients in the city and southwestern Ontario," said Moira Burke, managing partner in the London office. "Our success has been directly related to our ability to continue to attract, motivate and retain high-performance individuals. We recruit men and women who can't resist solving a problem. Our people, in turn, sustain the loyalty of our clients by providing them with creative solutions and services."

"London has gone through many changes and is repositioning itself to adapt to today's economic realities," she observed. "We're proud to play a role, as our firm has for more than 50 years, in identifying and encouraging a new wave of entrepreneurship to help London continue to grow and its people to prosper."

Ernst & Young also takes its community corporate citizenship seriously, encouraging its people to give freely of their time and energy to charitable, business and civic organizations. On a national scale, the London office is a strong partner in Ernst & Young's co-sponsorship of Canada's annual Entrepreneur of the Year awards to recognize successful business people.

From a modest beginning a half a century ago, Ernst & Young London's office is a proud participant in the community and a widely recognized contributor to the success of its clients. ▮▮

Situated in One London Place, Ernst & Young's team of dedicated professionals offers outstanding expertise to assist clients in managing their growth.

THE LONDON FREE PRESS

with the purchase of Sun Media Corp., Quebecor Inc. became the owners of *The Free Press*.

In many ways, *The Free Press* not only recorded progress and change in London and southwestern Ontario for a century and a half, it itself kept pace with the community and the times. In the age of information the newspaper continues to adopt new technology, adjust to the evolving needs of its customers and prepare for even more change in the future.

Computer technology and state-of-the-art publishing and distribution techniques make it possible for faster and more versatile production of *The Free Press*. The paper early on embraced the Internet wave and established its first website in 1996, making it easier for Londoners to interact with the news and debate the issues of the day.

"What we're seeing today in terms of new technology has in effect been a part of the newspaper business from the beginning," says Les Pyette, who in 2000 became *The Free Press* publisher. "We not only report the latest in technology advances, we plan very carefully to adapt the best ones that improve our product."

"At the same time, we are very much aware that modern technology is there to help us do our basic job better, to keep our readers up to date on world, Canadian and local events and to provide a forum for comment and debate. People take their newspaper very seriously and we in turn accept that it is our role to bring forward a wide variety of viewpoints so that informed decisions may be made."

The Free Press and the London area have come a long way since the newspaper's first hand-cranked press at a time when the city was a town of fewer than 4,000 people. Today's vibrant, bustling city one hundred times its size in 1849 is served by one of Canada's most successful regional dailies. The histories of the city and the newspaper continue intertwined as they've grown up together. ❦

T he London Free Press, serving London and southwestern Ontario for more than 150 years, is dedicated to publishing an accurate and credible daily newspaper for the people of London and the surrounding region. It is committed to reporting, interpreting and fairly commenting on, the people, events and facts of the community and the world at large in order to foster debate and promote change and growth.

Founded in 1849, *The London Free Press* is today as committed to its community as it was at its inception. *The Free Press* takes pride in the fact that over the years it has been unswerving in its promotion of the city and area, thriving on the successes of London's people, businesses and institutions.

The newspaper continues to believe it has a responsibility to not only chronicle and comment on the news of the day, but also to encourage and support the progress of the region. This is evident in the paper's historical approach to helping build a better London and to be a leading participant through sponsorships and initiatives on behalf of the city and its people.

Current examples include *The Free Press*' early commitment to the 2001 London Canada Summer Games, the exciting new Covent Garden Market and its ongoing support of the community's major cultural, learning and health institutions, particularly, The Grand Theatre, The London Health Sciences Centre and St. Joseph's Health Care Centre. This close involvement of the newspaper in helping make things better reflects a long-standing recognition that what is good for Londoners is ultimately beneficial to the health and future of *The Free Press*.

Originally founded as the weekly *Canadian Free Press* by Scottish printer William Sutherland on January 2, 1849, the newspaper was acquired in 1853 by Josiah Blackburn and turned into a daily two years later.

The Blackburn name was synonymous with *The Free Press* for the next 144 years as successive generations expanded the newspaper and built a local media empire. In 1997, Sun Media Corp. of Toronto acquired *The Free Press* and extensive changes in makeup and coverage followed with the launch of a Sunday edition a year later. In 1998,

(top) The London Free Press, *present day and, circa 1945 (bottom).*

CALLON   DIETZ

The land surveyor is one of the more unrecognized yet important persons in early Ontario. Indeed, pioneer surveyors from the 1800s were the first to set the stage on which Londoners now live.

"When I come across a surveyor's old stone monument while doing a new survey, and realize how accurate their work was using very rudimentary tools, I'm simply amazed," says Terry Dietz, owner of Callon Dietz Ontario Land Surveyors in London. "I feel a part of a very old and critically important legacy."

Established in London in 1967, Callon Dietz has a formidable history of providing land-surveying services in London and the surrounding area. Terry Dietz joined the firm in 1991 and became sole shareholder in 1994. In 1998, the firm achieved its ISO 9002 Quality System Standards designation for its comprehensive client service stance. Callon Dietz is one of the first land survey firms in Canada to achieve this designation.

Today, Callon Dietz provides services to a wide variety of projects including gas pipelines and other utilities, highway reconstruction programs, subdivision and lot surveys, digital terrain modeling and high-tech mapping. While London has been its base of operations, the firm increasingly does business throughout Ontario and is expanding to other countries.

"There are two keys to our success," says Terry. "We do extensive research to support our survey opinions. The other important factor, of course, is the skills and experience of our staff. Our people are knowledgeable, hardworking and diligent. We couldn't do it without them."

State-of-the-art technology also plays a key role in day-to-day operations at Callon Dietz. Where early surveyors used rudimentary equipment including the compass, steel measuring tape and telescopic transit, modern equipment provides the accuracy and speed essential for today's more complex projects.

Global Positioning System (GPS) receivers and electronic total station theodolites, for example, have dramatically decreased the time it takes to do surveys, while greatly increasing the accuracy of collected data. Data is then transferred to computer-assisted drafting programs that quickly produce digital survey maps, replacing the hand-drawn reports of past years.

Terry says he is often humbled to be a descendent in this legendary profession. "Surveying is like putting a jigsaw puzzle together. Many times the work we do is based upon maps and records prepared up to 200 years ago. Being able to accurately reconstruct the historical position of boundaries and help build new projects based on this work is very satisfying." ◀

(top) State-of-the-art instrumentation allows Callon Dietz to provide immediate and cost-effective services to its clients.

(right) Leading-edge software and enhancements assure Callon Dietz clients of accurate and prompt survey products.

LONDON ECONOMIC DEVELOPMENT CORPORATION

T he London Economic Development Corporation (LEDC) is a partnership between the City of London and the city's business community, with the aim of strengthening the community's business environment in order to improve the economic well-being of all Londoners.

"London has a dynamic and synergistic business environment that has consistently generated good and stable employment to a very capable and qualified work force," says John Kime, President and CEO of the LEDC. "Our job is to ensure that any business looking to expand, whether it's an existing company in London or one planning to establish in a new location, is fully aware of the qualities and strengths of our community."

The LEDC was established in 1997 as an independent, not-for-profit enterprise using private sector management principles to market London to global investors. Leading business and city representatives make up its Board of Directors, operating a private/public model for economic development similar to those in many major North American cities.

"In today's highly competitive industrial-development marketplace, it is important that business people making growth and expansion decisions are able to deal with people who speak their language and use an entrepreneurial approach," says Kime. "That's what we're able to do on behalf of London and it strikes a positive response among companies and organizations considering our city for investment."

London's historic Forks of the Thames and the downtown. Downtown office tower as seen from the core area Victoria Park.

London has historical strengths in health care, education, manufacturing, telecommunications and information technology, agricultural businesses and financial services. The LEDC is capitalizing on these strengths and targeting a priority list that includes the existing sectors plus focuses on emerging sectors such as biotechnology, high-tech manufacturing technology, transportation and distribution and many forms of e-commerce.

"One of our key strengths is our southwestern Ontario location, equal-distant between the Metro Toronto and Detroit regions," according to Kime. "There are more than 150 million consumers within a day's drive of London. We're on a major avenue of the NFTA Superhighway with excellent rail and air services giving businesses strategic access to both their customers and suppliers."

With both the renowned University of Western Ontario with its widely recognized Ivey School of Business and Fanshawe College in the community, London maintains a diverse and well-educated workforce that is attractive to employers. The city is also known for its tree-lined streets, green parks and friendly, hospitable population of close to 400,000, offering a much sought-after quality of life.

Given today's communication technology, London is a prime example of an attractive location where businesses can "work globally but live locally"—a key factor for recruitment and retention of skilled staff.

Check out the LEDC website at www.londonedc.com, and find out more about the LONDON ADVANTAGE. ◖

SPRIET ASSOCIATES

priet Associates has a distinguished history as an engineering and architectural services company in London, and today is recognized for its contributions to the design of many fine buildings, facilities, offices, community halls and arenas in southwestern Ontario.

As with many successful companies, the story begins with the energy and initiative of one business leader—Andrew (Andy) Spriet, P. Eng. In 1961, after working with a London engineering consulting firm in the design of sewage works, he struck out on his own, focusing on municipal engineering projects in the region. His fledging firm quickly established a reputation for design expertise on drains, bridges and culverts and his first major building project was the former Ivanhoe Curling Club in London.

He was shortly joined by his cousin, Anthony (Tony) DeVos, P. Eng., and the two specialized in rural drainage projects which became the cornerstone and continue today as a major activity for Spriet Associates. Today, Spriet Associates employs some 30 people in London and Sudbury. Eleven have degrees in engineering, four are professional architects and the remainder are highly skilled technicians, technologists and support personnel.

Through the drainage work being done for municipalities, the engineering firm built strong business relationships with municipal councils and staff, opening up other opportunities for engineering and architectural contracts. In subsequent years, professional engineers Daniel (Danny) Young, John Spriet,

Larry Gigun and Kevin McLlmurray, joined the growing company and more recently a new generation of young engineers, Tony DeVos's son Michael and John Spriet's son John Michael have become members of the team.

The firm is known for a broad area of specialty including drainage, municipal services, roadwork and bridge construction and architecture, with architecture playing an increasing role. The nucleus for the expansion in this area has been architects Norman Kroetsch and Paul Loreto.

A particular specialty is design for local arenas and, as well, the company has many commercial, industrial and design/build contractors as clients. The design/build business involves a close working relationship with its subsidiary Norlon Builders London Limited.

"Our practice is best described as local, quality-driven, economical and practical," says Andy Spriet. "Our client base is predominately with municipalities within a 60 mile radius from our two offices. This proximity allows quick and efficient service to our customers. We're proud of our track record and client list which are the envy of many competitors."

"The new millennium and a robust economy bring great promise for our firm's continuing role in the growth and prosperity of the London community, which we consider to be our home." ∎

(above) *Burlington Twin Pad Arena.*

(right) *Management Group: From left, Kevin McLlmurray, Larry Gigun, Andy Spriet, Danny Young, Tony DeVos and John Spriet.*

N O R L O N   B U I L D E R S
L O N D O N   L I M I T E D

N orlon Builders London Limited has developed a well-deserved reputation over more than 25 years as a quality construction firm, and particularly as an early leader in the design/build business.

A subsidiary of A.M. Spriet & Associates, Norlon is one of London's more prominent construction companies for commercial, industrial and institutional clients. The engineering and architectural expertise in the Spriet firm and quality construction performance by Norlon has proven to be a winning combination.

In recent years, the firm has been active in the design and construction of arenas and recreational facilities in southern Ontario, with two noteworthy projects being the $10-million University of Western Ontario stadium, as part of the London Alliance 2001 Canada Summer Games, and an $11-million arena complex in Leamington, Ontario.

Norlon was founded in 1976 as the concept of design/build was gaining popularity. This process allows an investor or company to describe a potential building project, and have Norlon prepare preliminary plans and cost estimates. This gives the client a design and a firm price for construction without incurring costs until the plan is accepted and goes forward. This method of contracting out work is in particular favour with non-public investors. While the original activity of Norlon was in the design/build field—and it is still a leader here—the company now bids on many public construction tender calls.

Norlon has become a leading London-area construction company with eight office staff and numerous field specialists. Wolfgang Ginzel, Vice-President, Contract Administration, and Maurice DeMaiter, P. Eng., Vice-President, Construction Administration, manage the day-to-day operations of the firm along with Ms. Linda Lauzon, CMA, as Comptroller.

The company credits its continuing success to repeat business with its clients. An example would be The University of Western Ontario where Norlon has undertaken many building renovations on the campus. Recent examples of notable design/build projects are the Burlington Twin Pad Arena, the Strathroy Twin Pad Arena and the Trudell Medical building and manufacturing plant in London.

One of the company's greatest strengths is its ability to perform on time and on budget due to the dedication of its skilled staff.

Norlon is proud to call London home and finds the city an excellent base of operations, particularly because of the availability of quality construction workers in all building trades. ◀

(above) Trudell Medical, Offices and Warehouse, London, Ontario.

(below) Canada Games 2001 Stadium.

NEAL, PALLETT & TOWNSEND LLP

N eal, Pallett & Townsend LLP, is a unique firm of chartered accountants. The stately Victorian home that houses its offices has a traditional and old-world appearance, but the innovative

Business advisory services are focused to give private business clients added strength and stability, thus helping them maximize income as they pursue their business objectives. The firm is proud of the fact that many of its clients have depended on individual partners for over 20 years, testament to an ability to quickly address clients' needs for more than just traditional services.

As well as being able to meet professional needs of their clients, the partners of Neal, Pallett & Townsend LLP always maintain a human side to their client relationships. When there's time for a break they can be found spending time serving on the boards of local charities, on the golf course, or on the ice playing hockey or curling with staff and associates. While one may be engrossed in a hand of bridge, another will be found on the open road riding a Harley with clients and friends. By being close to their clients, the partners and staff of Neal, Pallett & Townsend LLP have developed and maintained the special client relationships that are an underlying reason for the firm's success. ◗

approach taken in its service to clients is anything but. The six partners who created this firm draw upon their individual and specialized knowledge to address specific client situations. Working with a full complement of highly trained professional staff, they capitalize on these individuals' expertise to create teams uniquely suited to each client's needs.

The partners of Neal, Pallett & Townsend LLP recognize that entrepreneurial business owners and professionals need specific business advice if they are to react quickly in today's environment of electronic commerce. Employing a targeted team approach, the firm is structured to quickly assist clients with strategic business negotiations and planning, financing proposals, business valuations and due diligence work in purchase negotiations. With experience in such specialized areas as litigation support, business operational assessment, corporate reorganization and dispute resolution through mediation and arbitration, clients can be assured of uniquely suitable assistance.

One partner has an M.B.A. degree from the distinguished Richard Ivey School of Business; another has provided specialized advice to the health-care industry for over 20 years, and is a member of the Canadian Federation of Financial Planners. The firm is a member of the National Association of Forensic Accountants, which demands a high degree of special skills. Of course, traditional accounting services are also provided— indeed, the firm has a reputation for first-rate Canadian and U.S. tax advice and estate planning.

Pictured from left are the partners of Neal, Pallett & Townsend LLP.
(Above) L.J. Sandy Wetstein, Barrie J. Neal and John D.R. Prueter.
(Below) Jonathan R. Townsend, Glenn J. Hardman and David J. Pallett.

Photo by Mike Grandmaison

Health Care, Education
and Quality of Life

Photo by Mike Grandmaison

LONDON HEALTH SCIENCES CENTRE

L ondon Health Sciences Centre, renowned not only across Canada but around the world, is a major contributor to the city's historic reputation as a leader in medical health care, teaching and research.

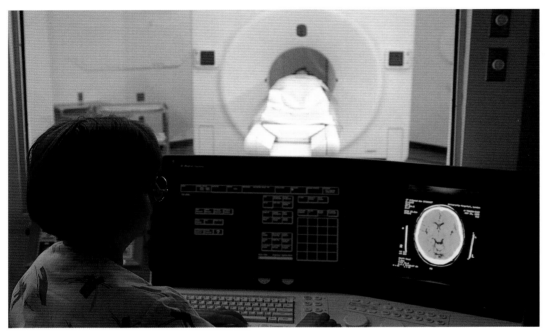

Dedicated to excellence in patient care, teaching and research, London Health Sciences Centre has a capacity of 776 beds and 38 bassinets. The staff of 7,237 care for more than 700,000 inpatient, outpatient and emergency patients annually.

Spread over 3 million square feet of property, London Health Sciences Centre is located on two campuses at three sites. The University Campus is on Windemere Road adjacent to the University of Western Ontario, the Victoria Campus is situated on South Street as well as on Commissioners Road. London Health Sciences Centre also has two community health centers, the Byron Family Medical Centre and the Victoria Family Medical Centre.

The medical-care facilities offered by London Health Sciences Centre are both comprehensive and noteworthy. Widely known for excellence in general medicine, including family medicine, surgical and anaesthetic services, it also includes a number of clinical programs that have achieved provincial, and in some cases, national and international recognition. These include clinical neurological services, critical care and trauma services, cardiac care, cancer care, multi-organ transplantation, women's health, medical imaging and MRI, reproductive medicine and orthopaedic/sports medicine.

The Cardiac Care Program at London Health Sciences Centre is the largest provider of comprehensive adult and paediatric cardiac services in Canada with about 100,000 patients a year benefiting from the Centre's leading edge approach to cardiac care. Upwards of 1,700 open-heart surgeries are performed annually, and in 1999 the world's first closed-chest, robotic-assisted beating-heart coronary-artery bypass graft was carried out. This historic event is an excellent example of the bringing together of medical research and treatment available at London Health Sciences

Centre. It is expected that in the future up to 25 per cent of heart-bypass procedures will use the closed-chest, robotic-assisted techniques thereby decreasing length of stay in hospital, lessening patient trauma and pain and speeding recovery.

Another significant component of London Health Sciences Centre is the Children's Hospital of Western Ontario. Its Paediatric Emergency Department is the only facility of its kind between Toronto and Winnipeg and each year more than 30,000 children are assessed by its staff, including those children admitted to the Paediatric Critical Care Unit for the critically ill.

London Health Sciences Centre is also widely recognized as a leader in women's health care. Its maternal/newborn service is family focused, offering one-on-one nursing, around-the-clock obstetrical consultant coverage and co-operative affiliations with midwives. More than 2,200 babies are born at the Centre annually. The Department of Gynaecology and Reproductive Medicine is internationally known for its excellence in Reproductive Endocrinology and Infertility, offering a wide range of services. The Women's Health Care Centre encourages patients to participate in their care, while the Gynaecologic Oncology focuses on informed choice in cancer care. The Breast Management Clinic ensures no woman referred to the clinic waits more than six days for an appointment.

While its primary commitment is patient care, the Centre ensures health-care excellence to future generations through its emphasis on teaching and research with affiliations to more than 60 regional schools and institutions including the University of Western Ontario Faculty of Medicine and Dentistry and the Robarts Research Institute.

As an academic health sciences centre, research is fundamental in the ability of London Health Sciences Centre to provide the best in patient care, and to attract and retain excellent scientists and physicians. Significant research and innovation initiatives are coordinated through London Health Sciences Centre Research Inc., which supports a working partnership among other major institutions

including The Robarts Research Institute, The University of Western Ontario, the Lawson Research Institute, the Child Health Research Institute and the London Regional Cancer Centre.

"We are going through a lot of change, but we've experienced considerable change and evolution in the more than a century we've served London," says Tony Dagnone, President and CEO. "We know that our primary focus must always be care of the patient with an emphasis on learning and discovery. The commitment and support of our staff, our physicians and our communities have been integral to our success in the past and will continue to be as vital in the future."

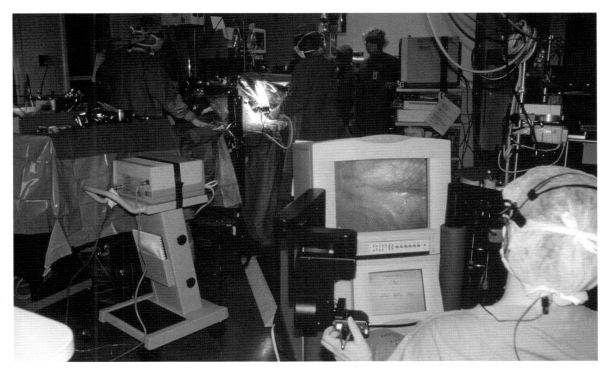

While London Health Sciences Centre reaches out around the world, it also exercises its mandate for clinical strategic linkages with other hospitals across southwestern Ontario and in northern Ontario areas. This program of clinical integration improves access to health care in regional communities and provides specialized expertise not readily available.

With the arrival of the new millennium, London Health Sciences Centre is itself undergoing major renewal through a comprehensive building, renovation and restructuring program to enhance health-care services for the future. The program, mandated by Ontario's Health Services Restructuring Commission, is part of the largest infrastructure project in London's history and one of the biggest in Ontario. At London Health Sciences Centre it will add more modern patient care and work areas, improve patient accessibility and provide the capability to treat an increased number of patients.

The modernization and improvements being made over five years will ensure that London Health Sciences Centre will maintain its primary and traditional commitment to excellence in patient care. As part of the restructuring program, the Centre is closing its antiquated South Street site, the original Victoria Hospital. The project will consolidate all city emergency care for children and adults at the University and Victoria campuses, with an expected 60,000 additional visits annually. ◄

ST. JOSEPH'S HEALTH CARE LONDON

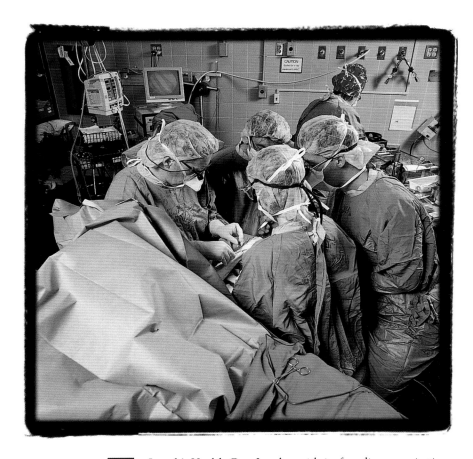

S t. Joseph's Health Care London with its founding organizations has a distinguished legacy of service to the London community, Southwestern Ontario and the Veterans of Canada. Today's new organization is poised for the future in health care.

As an integral part of London hospital renewal, Parkwood Hospital and in the near future, the London/St. Thomas Psychiatric Hospital, join with St. Joseph's Hospital, Mount Hope Centre for Long Term Care and a host of community-based programs to form St. Joseph's Health Care London.

"At St. Joseph's, we are looking forward to the next era in health care," states Cliff Nordal, President and CEO. "The hospital system we are building today will meet the needs of generations to come. We are changing, but our new growth comes from strong roots and a core commitment to our vision and values of respect, excellence and compassion."

(above) Advances in technology, less invasive (keyhole) surgical procedures, and new anaesthetic agents have contributed to the growing number of ambulatory care procedures being done at St. Joseph's.

(right) St. Joseph's is one of only two lithotripsy units in the province, with more than 2,700 patients coming from all over Ontario each year for treatment. St. Joseph's recently installed a new lithotripter which provides more flexibility and greater effectiveness than its 10-year-old predecessor.

Mount Hope Centre for Long Term Care was originally opened by the Sisters of St. Joseph in 1869 as an orphanage. St. Joseph's Hospital followed in 1888, and in 1894, the Women's Christian Association of London founded Parkwood Hospital. Facilities and services including The HIV Care Programme; St. Joseph's Family Medical and Dental Centre; and the Withdrawal Management Centre are part of the St. Joseph's family. In the future, new facilities for specialized mental health care will be built in London and St. Thomas.

St. Joseph's is owned by the St. Joseph's Health Care Society of the Roman Catholic Diocese of London and is governed by a volunteer board of directors representing the community. The organization is a major teaching and research centre affiliated with the University of Western Ontario and Fanshawe College. The Lawson Research Institute has grown to become internationally recognized for research advancements in a variety of areas including newborn health, diagnostic imaging techniques, chronic disease and rehabilitation. Students from a range of other provincial and national education institutions also avail themselves of St. Joseph's strong clinical and research programs.

The health centre employs more than 4,000 staff members and benefits from the contributions of more than 1,700 volunteers.

With the rebuilding of London's hospital system comes significant new roles for St. Joseph's in the next four to five years. St. Joseph's Hospital, located on Grosvenor Street, will see the expansion of its role in day surgery, treatment and illness-prevention programs with the evolution of an ambulatory care centre and a family birthing centre. The new hospital will include current centres in urology, hand and upper limb surgery, and diabetes. Eye care will be expanded to house city-wide ophthalmology care, including the Ivey Eye Institute. Approximately 40 inpatient beds will serve the new family birthing centre and the surgery programs, permitting hospital stays of up to 72 hours as needed. A full range of diagnostic services including MRIs and CT scans will continue to support care focused

on health and healing through prevention and treatment.

Parkwood Hospital continues its leadership roles in rehabilitation, complex care, palliative care and geriatrics. Inpatient rehabilitation services from across the city will move to Parkwood to create a rehabilitation institute for London and Southwestern Ontario. Specialized rehabilitation services include: spinal cord injury, acquired brain injury, stroke, hip fractures and amputation. Day programs and outpatient services will continue to expand to support people returning to home and community living. Parkwood also continues its distinguished care for veterans.

St. Joseph's will also play a leadership role in the transformation of local and regional mental health services as the province of Ontario divests itself from direct management of provincial psychiatric hospitals. New facilities for specialized mental health services will be built beside Parkwood Hospital and in St. Thomas, near the current psychiatric hospital setting. Continued provincial investment in new community programs to support successful home living will occur before the current psychiatric hospitals close.

"We have a once-in-a-lifetime opportunity to rebuild our system for generations to come. Medical advancements now mean that more than 80 per cent of hospital-related treatments are conducted on an outpatient basis. The scope and significance of the changes for St. Joseph's means we are poised for this continuing future trend," notes Mr. Nordal. "At the same time, the future holds many opportunities for us to engage in new partnerships with communities and organizations."

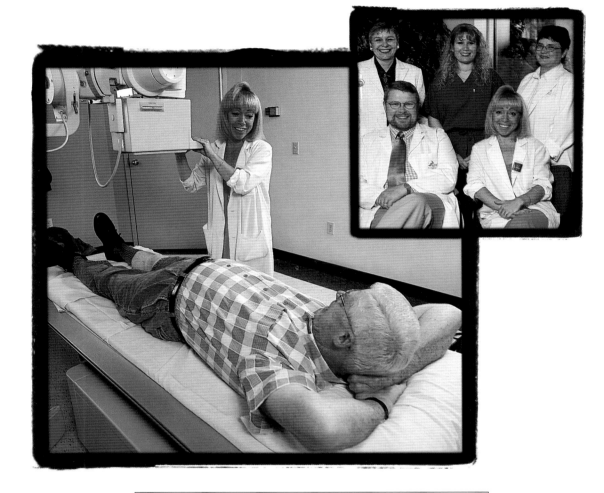

(above) St. Joseph's is offering extended ambulatory care options to the community through its new satellite imaging suite, one of the first of its kind in Ontario. Those requiring an x-ray or ultrasound now have the option of obtaining St. Joseph's services and expertise in a community setting.

(left) Each day, a virtual legion of volunteers walks our hallways, visits patients at their bedsides, helps residents enjoy their recreational time and makes our families and visitors feel more at home.

An important factor for the new St. Joseph's is the continuing support of the St. Joseph's and Parkwood Hospital Foundations. The foundations provide a critical link between care, research and the community. Through donor support, the foundations contribute to research initiatives, equipment and advancements in care delivery, and capital funds to support hospital building projects. "We simply could not sustain our current activities and rebuild for the future without the support of our foundations," adds Mr. Nordal.

Based on a common history of identifying needs in the community and finding ways to meet them, St. Joseph's Health Care London continues its vision of being a respected source of excellent health service, guided by the people we serve, provided by people who care. ⁍

THE UNIVERSITY OF WESTERN ONTARIO

The University of Western Ontario is a vibrant centre of learning with 1,250 faculty members and more than 26,000 undergraduate and graduate students.

part-time faculty and staff and an annual payroll of more than $267 million. Combined faculty, staff and student spending through Western contributes more than $1 billion in economic benefit annually to the London community—indirectly sustaining more than 10,000 jobs in the area.

Research is an integral part of Western, and external support for research projects totals approximately $85 million a year—making it one of Canada's top 10 research universities. More than 2,000 research projects are currently underway on campus, ranging from medical and scientific research to policy studies in social science and creative work in the arts and humanities.

There are six major libraries with more than six million books, audiovisual materials and microforms. Together, they constitute one of the largest research library systems in Canada.

Many of the more than 1,250 faculty members are world leaders in their disciplines. Western's professors are known both for their teaching skills and their research and regularly receive provincial, national and international achievement awards.

"We're proud of our campus and the outstanding facilities, but we're prouder still that Western is a renowned centre of discovery and intellectual adventure," says Paul Davenport, Western's president. "We attract outstanding students and faculty from across Canada and around the world who come to Western because they want the best education possible."

"Western, above all, has a tradition of fostering an atmosphere of discovery, inquiry and personal and academic development. At its heart, a university is about people—our contribution to teaching, research and society is determined by the people who work and study here."

Western's 170,000 graduates live and work throughout Canada and around the world—making Alumni Western the second-largest alumni association in the country.

As it moves into the new millennium, The University of Western Ontario maintains its dedication to the advancement of quality learning through teaching and research and the application of knowledge in order to superbly serve the interests of London, Canada and society. ▮

The University of Western Ontario, founded in London in 1878, today is a vibrant centre of learning with 1,250 faculty members and more than 26,000 undergraduate and graduate students. Through its 12 faculties and schools and three affiliated colleges, the university offers more than 50 different degree and diploma programs—bringing the prestige of world-class achievement in education and research to the city.

The rolling, heavily treed campus spreads over 155 hectares of land along the banks of the Thames River, making it a favourite "must see" for visitors to London. Western's many historic limestone buildings combine with newer, architecturally attractive structures to create a pleasing setting for teaching, learning and research.

Well-known facilities, many of which are regularly used by the community, include the McIntosh Gallery, the Hume Cronyn Memorial Observatory, the University of Western Ontario Research Park, Spencer Hall Conference Centre, Windermere Manor Conference Centre, Talbot Theatre, Alumni Hall, the 3M Centre, the Thompson Recreation and Athletic Centre and the University Community Centre. In 2000 a new multi-use stadium will open as a major community venue on campus.

Western is the city's second largest employer with more than 3,500 full-time and 2,100

Research is an integral part of Western. More than 2,000 research projects are currently underway, ranging from medical and scientific research to policy studies in social science and creative work in the arts and humanities.

FANSHAWE COLLEGE

F anshawe College, one of the largest among Ontario community colleges, is recognized for its flexible and innovative curriculum, the leading position of its co-op programs and a historical commitment to community participation. Fanshawe has more than 12,000 full-time and 36,000 part-time registrants annually, and current surveys report that 92 percent of its graduates from full-time programs are employed within six months of graduating.

While its main campus is in northeast London, Fanshawe is a provider of quality education and training to residents of the four counties of Middlesex, Norfolk, Elgin and Oxford. Satellite campuses are situated in Simcoe, St. Thomas and Woodstock, and education centres in Tillsonburg and Strathroy. Together, the college operates in 20 cities and towns in southwestern Ontario.

The college's London location, offering the best of friendly, small-town living with ready access to larger centres along the Montreal-Toronto-Detroit corridor, positions Fanshawe as the first choice among Ontario college applicants. A full range of services and programs also attracts Fanshawe students. They include state-of-the-art computer labs, Internet access and personal e-mail addresses, video conference capabilities, a library and resource centre, cafeterias and restaurants, a clothing/gift store, book and computer store, intramural and varsity sports programs, and a newly opened on-campus residence and conference centre which offers furnished suites accommodating 392 students.

A 4,050-square-metre fitness centre is well used by both students and members of the London community. Students with learning disabilities may also receive support from the newly established Millennium Centre, which provides counselling, learning strategies, technological and assistive learning devices and mentoring.

Fanshawe offers an integrated, broadly based curriculum, meeting the learning needs of people in all parts of the education spectrum. Students may enroll in one-, two- or three-year full-time programs, while many thousands are attracted to the popular apprenticeship and part-time continuing education programs. For students not fully prepared to enter a career or enroll in full-time courses, preparatory and academic upgrading are also available, including the English as a second language option that attracts many overseas students.

The quality and diversity of Fanshawe programs attract students from not only Ontario but from across Canada and more than 30 foreign countries. 70,000 alumni are a strong testament to the continued success of the college.

While the majority of its students are from Ontario, Fanshawe attracts enrollment from across Canada and 30 foreign countries.

A series of post-graduate programs attracts those with university degrees who seek practical career training. Fanshawe continues to expand its agreements with universities to allow its students to transfer their credits for degree studies, and more than 18 universities in Canada, the United States and Australia now accept Fanshawe student accreditation.

To enhance the study experience and prepare students for their chosen career, many Fanshawe programs include co-operative education placement, field trips and independent study opportunities. Fanshawe provides the highest number of co-operative education options in the Canadian community college system—more than 30 undergraduate programs offer co-op placements.

"We're proud of the quality and diversity of our educational programs, and the continued success of our more than 70,000 alumni," says President Howard Rundle. "Significant credit for our ongoing ability to deliver learning and training that matches the ever changing needs of our students goes to our outstanding faculty of 400 full-time and over 1,000 part-time teachers, as well as our highly committed support and administrative staff."

Fanshawe's slogan is "Community Driven . . . Student Focused." Its current theme is helping people soar—to achieve their personal best at any time in their life. London and southwestern Ontario take flight as a result. ▮

The London Campus of Fanshawe College is situated on 100 landscaped acres. Facilities include computer labs, library, gymnasiums, a community fitness centre and a student residence with significant growth planned over the next several years.

F I F T E E N

The Marketplace, Hospitality and Attractions

Photo by Mike Grandmaison

HILTON
LONDON ONTARIO

From their rooms, guests can see all parts of London and appreciate the beauty of the community spread around the forks of the Thames River.

Opened originally in 1975 as a Holiday Inn, the Hilton London has traditionally been recognized as the hospitality centre for southwestern Ontario. In 1998, the hotel was acquired by Royal Host Real Estate Investment Trust (REIT) of Calgary. Its wholly owned subsidiary Royal Host Corp. manages Hilton London, which is one of its 75 hotels and resort properties in Canada, the United States and Mexico.

By car, the Hilton London is reached from the 401 corridor via Wellington Road. London International Airport is 20 minutes by regular limousine service, and the Via Train station is a four-block cab ride away.

When arriving at the King Street entrance of the Hilton, guests know immediately this is going to be an outstanding and satisfying experience. They are welcomed by door attendants dressed in distinctive Beefeater attire. These attendants set the stage for every visit, reminding guests of the historical links of London to its founding in 1793 by Lieutenant Colonel John Graves Simcoe, the first lieutenant governor of Upper Canada.

The swish of the automatic doors opens up to the lobby with luxurious marble and carpets that denote the style and attention to detail throughout the Hilton London Ontario. Carefully selected and trained staff promptly completes registration for each guest in the room of their choice. Express check-in and checkout are convenient services for those in a hurry.

All rooms have been newly renovated and wonderfully appointed. The housekeeping staff takes pride in preparing a home away from home and makes an extra effort to ensure it is ready in all respects. For those selecting accommodation on the Business Class Floors, there is private keyed access and use of the business class lounge. All guest rooms are equipped with an electronic key access system. A number of rooms are equipped for persons with disabilities.

T he Hilton London Ontario is much more than a hotel. It's a city landmark, a preeminent community meeting and conference centre, a favourite dining and entertainment destination and the crossroads to downtown and the London Convention Centre.

Soaring upward 22 floors, the Hilton London offers 322 spacious guest rooms, including attractive suites and the business-convenient Hilton HHonors floors, making it the city's largest hotel. Two opulent top floor suites, the Prime Minister and the Executive, are popular for special occasions.

Ideally situated in the heart of London's business, shopping and entertainment district, the hotel overlooks The Forest City with its trademark trees in the many parks and along the streets and avenues.

(right) A warm welcome awaits all of The Hilton London's guests.

Each room features coffee-maker, hair dryer, iron and ironing board, in-room safe, remote controlled 25-inch television with on-command movies, and two separate telephone lines with guest voice mail, two data ports for laptop Internet access and a hands-free telephone.

Guest features also include complimentary access to the popular health club, which offers an indoor swimming pool, glass front sauna, whirlpool and fitness equipment to tone up after travel or relax with the family. Same-day valet laundry and dry cleaning services are added conveniences.

In the morning, a complimentary newspaper awaits each guest at their door. Now is the time to enjoy the daily buffet breakfast in the 90-seat Market Café on the second floor, or select from the room service menu with all-day selections. The Café features Continental and European cuisine and is also a popular spot for partaking of the a la carte lunch and dinner menu.

The adjacent award-winning London Grill has an established reputation for fine service and exquisitely prepared food for lunch and dinner. It features a la carte selections of Continental and Californian Fusion cuisine and is a favourite meeting spot in London for business, entertaining or that special occasion.

J. J. Keys Lounge just outside the London Grill is another favorite in London. Featuring casual lunches and light snacks, the inviting lounge and piano bar attracts both guests and visitors who are royally entertained with regular live entertainment. "Meet you at JJs" is an invitation for meeting and greeting in a relaxed atmosphere.

The meeting and banquet facilities, including the largest ballroom in southwestern Ontario, are a key hotel attraction. Situated on the second floor, the banqueting and meeting rooms may be reached from

(above) Indoor pool.

(below) London Grill Restaurant.

the lobby by both escalators and elevators or by the direct skyway to and from the London Convention Centre across King Street. The ballroom in its various size configurations, along with nearby meeting rooms, can provide up to 17 separate locations for meetings, presentations, receptions or banquets, with a total of 26,000 square feet available.

The Grand Ballroom capacity is up to 1,000 banquet style or 1,300 theatre style. Over the years the hotel has been the scene of major conventions, political gatherings, stylish receptions, business meetings and special family occasions including weddings and anniversaries. The convenient access to the Convention Centre gives London the combined size of facilities to easily handle the largest of sessions.

State-of-the-art audio visual equipment services are available on-site 24 hours day, and freight elevators opening directly into the ballroom allow the convenient moving in of display and other materials. Set up for exhibits, the ballroom accommodates up to 75 booths and is utilized by companies and organizations from all parts of Canada.

(top) *Victoria and Albert Room.*

(bottom) *Windsor Club Room.*

Guests and visitors have the convenience of 228 covered and heated parking spaces with additional generous parking within easy walking distance.

The Hilton is a convenient base for guests to explore nearby entertainment spots, taste the cuisine of the city's finest restaurants and visit the many and varied retail stores, including those in the Galleria Shopping Centre. London's treasured Grand Theatre is also within walking distance, where live professional plays highlight the theatre season. Also in season are performances of Orchestra London at Centennial Hall, 10 blocks north of the hotel.

If guests enjoy walking or cycling, the Thames Valley network offers many miles of delightful meandering pathways easily reached at the forks of the river three blocks to the west.

The Hilton is a favourite stopping off point and operating base for business travelers, as London is halfway between Toronto and Windsor/Detroit. It's also popular with families visiting the many attractions of the region, including the nearby Great Lakes and the world-famous Stratford Shakespearean Festival.

"When you add it all up, our central location, the quality of our facilities and the variety of services available, you can see why we are proud of the Hilton London Ontario," says hotel General Manager Joe Drummond. "But in the hospitality business, bricks and mortar, along with convenient and attractive amenities, are only the starting point. What sets us apart is guest and customer loyalty, and you must earn that through the service you provide."

"Only people make the difference. You can have the most modern and spectacular facility, but it's the people you recruit and train who make it breathe and shine. There are three words that describe what we do: passion, pride and caring."

Mr. Drummond describes the Hilton staff of more than 200 as made up of many individuals, each with specialized skills, but all members of a dedicated team, a team where each and every job is equal in value to all others, and each is a link in the hospitality chain.

"Each staff member makes a contribution based upon not only the training we provide, but also from his or her own determination to do the very best on behalf of the customer. Our mission is to create a 'wow' from the people who come to stay with us. We never think of ourselves as merely providing a place to sleep."

He believes that building a relationship with the customer is made up of every part of the service provided, from greeting and check-in, through the cleanliness and ambiance of the room and to the friendliness and "can do" attitude of everyone with whom the customer comes in contact.

"It all has to be seamless. We are successful when the customer's visit leaves him or her with a comfortable and pleasurable feeling. If there are problems, our job is to solve them immediately if not sooner."

Mr. Drummond says a critical part of the continuing success of the Hilton is that each staff associate has the confidence to carry out his

(right) Deluxe Guest Room.

or her job, secure that they are empowered to place customer service as their personal priority.

"London is a beautiful and vibrant city. Our job as the leader in the community's hospitality industry is to deliver the best possible experience. When we do that successfully, people will not only come back to stay at the Hilton and enjoy our facilities, but will also gain an outstanding impression of London as a community in which to live and do business." ◄

BEST WESTERN LAMPLIGHTER INN

F or more than 25 years, the Best Western Lamplighter Inn has welcomed travelers entering London on vacation, family visits and business. Located on Wellington Road, just north of Highway 401 and conveniently located across the road from Victoria Hospital, the Inn's distinctive domed restaurant is a well-known landmark referenced by both visitors and local residents alike when the directions are, "Meet me at the Lamplighter."

With 126 rooms including suites and mini-suites, the Best Western Lamplighter Inn coddles guests in a wide array of spacious and comforting accommodations. Suite service options include king-sized beds and double Jacuzzi whirlpool baths plus the living comfort and convenience of a mini kitchen and richly finished furnishings for in-room dining, conference or lounging.

The Lamplighter offers specially designed rooms for the physically challenged as well as specifically designated non-smoking accommodation. Pet friendly rooms are also available.

Long renowned for its quality accommodations and attentive and cheerful staff, the Lamplighter is poised for major expansion, which will add 72 rooms, suites and a year-round, glass-roofed indoor pool and waterslide area.

The architecturally soaring glass roof will open to the summer sun and close to seal out weather not welcome in a luxurious resort environment. A new, fully equipped exercise facility, adjacent to the pool, will offer guests at the Best Western Lamplighter Inn the opportunity to begin or end the day with their choice of everything from light exercise right up to a serious on-the-road workout.

Widely recognized as London's Hospitality Headquarters, the Lamplighter offers an impeccably appointed ballroom and banquet seating for 10 to 500. Its professional catering manager and staff ensure no detail is overlooked and no task left undone. The polished blend of personal service-experienced staff and uncompromising hospitality make the Lamplighter the premier choice for weddings, banquets and corporate functions.

With flexible meeting facilities, professional meeting planning assistance, state-of-the-art AV equipment and on-site technical support, the Lamplighter is a favourite meeting place for business and first choice for business meeting planners.

At the Best Western Lamplighter Inn, everyone on staff understands the importance of each guest's visit. It shows in every aspect of their painstaking attention to detail and their uncompromising commitment to do it right.

The Best Western Lamplighter Inn—London's Hospitality Headquarters. ◀

WESTERN FAIR
ASSOCIATION

The Western Fair is as old as Canada and throughout its history, has earned an international reputation for its leadership as an agricultural and social institution. Despite dramatic and often debilitating circumstances, the Fair has survived, prospered and met the challenge of change created by wars, economic recessions, crop failures, fires, competition, changing technologies, public tastes and attitudes.

Each year of operations brings the Association Directors opportunities to draw on new ideas, new thoughts, new methods and new inventions. By embracing the idea of progress and promoting human ingenuity and innovation, the Fair and the community which it serves have benefited in tangible ways.

Soon after its establishment at Queen's Park in 1887, Western Fair began to identify itself as much more than a one-event organization. Seed fairs, sportsmen's shows, carnivals, banquets, concerts, industrial trade conventions, theatre groups, schools and a host of other organizations use the facilities at Queen's Park throughout the year. New ventures such as the Home and Garden Show introduced in the spring of 1954, the Western Fair Raceway in 1961 and the Farm Show in 1962 are just examples of the Association's diversity and growth.

By the early 1970s more than 1.25 million visitors used the fairgrounds annually and Western Fair Association could proudly claim to be London's largest tourist attraction. Other ventures included the Youth Talent event, introduced in 1981, and an innovative approach to agricultural awareness with the award winning Rural Route Discovery program a decade later.

In 1996, the Western Fair opened its giant-screen IMAX theatre, introducing London audiences to bigger-than-life high-precision sound and breathtaking imagery for the first time. More than 30,000 school children are entertained, educated and enthralled by IMAX films every year. Just two years after the IMAX opening, the fair board passed a motion to proceed with the installation of slot machines at the race tracks. A portion of the lower floor of the grandstand and lower paddock facility have been leased to the Ontario Lottery Corporation and now house a very popular slot lounge. Proceeds from

> The 10-day exhibition held annually in September is the Fair's signature event, showcasing entertainment, achievement and excitement and drawing close to 300,000 visitors each year.

Western Fair Racetrack Slots are used to help support live racing and re-investment in the fairgrounds' plant and facilities.

The 10-day exhibition held annually in September is the Fair's signature event, showcasing entertainment, achievement and excitement and drawing close to 300,000 visitors each year. Spending as a result of the 1999 Western Fair generated a total of nearly $15 million in economic activity in Ontario, including about $10.5 million in London itself. Almost $4.5 million of this activity was converted into wages and salaries for citizens of Ontario, including $3.4 million for residents of London. In Ontario, 214.6 full-year jobs were supported by spending associated with the Western Fair and of those, 183.6 full-year jobs were in London. In addition, $2.48 million in taxes for all levels of government was generated as a result of the event.

Today's Western Fair Association is a sophisticated and multi-dimensional entity. It strives to excel in creating unique experiences that fulfil the ever changing entertainment and educational interests of the communities it serves. The Western Fair and its many supporters and sponsors have proven by embracing change that the London area can continue to move forward to a brighter and more prosperous future. This goal inspired the founders of the Association in 1868 when the Fair launched its first two-day fall fair event, and it is still relevant today. ◄

> In 1996, the Western Fair opened its giant-screen IMAX theatre, introducing London audiences to bigger-than-life high-precision sound and breathtaking imagery for the first time.

E N T E R P R I S E   I N D E X

The London Free Press
369 York Street
London, Ontario N6A 4G1
Phone: 519-679-1111
Fax: 519-667-5520
E-mail: dzetts@lfpress.com
www.lfpress.com
Page 125

London Health Sciences Centre
P.O. Box 5375
London, Ontario
Phone: 519-685-8500
Fax: 519-667-6797
www.lhsc.on.ca
Pages 134-135

London Hydro
111 Horton Street
London, Ontario N6A 4H6
Phone: 519-661-5503
Fax: 519-661-5052
www.londonhydro.com
Page 102

LONDONCONNECT
111 Horton Street
London, Ontario N6A 4H6
Phone: 519-661-5800 ext. 4525
Fax: 519-661-5052
E-mail: lcsales@londonhydro.com
www.londonconnect.on.ca
Page 103

McCormick Canada
316 Rectory Street
London, Ontario N5W 3V9
Phone: 519-432-1166
Fax: 519-432-4779
E-mail: angie-francolini@mccormick.com
Pages 100-101

Microtronix Systems Ltd.
955 Green Valley Road
London, Ontario N6N 1E4
Phone: 519-649-4900
Fax: 519-649-0355
E-mail: kauzins@microtronix.ca
www.microtronix.ca
Pages 110-111

Neal, Pallett & Townsend LLP
289 Dufferin Avenue
London, Ontario N6B 1Z1
Phone: 519-432-5534
Fax: 519-432-6544
E-mail: info@nptca.com
Page 130

Norlon Builders London Limited
151 York Street
London, Ontario N6A 1A8
Phone: 519-672-7590
Fax: 519-645-6989
E-mail: norlon@on.aibn.com
www.norlon.com
Page 129

OES, Inc.
4056 Blakie Road
London, Ontario N6L 1P7
Phone: 519-652-5833
Fax: 519-652-3795
E-mail: oes@oes-inc.com
www.oes-inc.com
Page 114

Rho-Can
770 Industrial Road
London, Ontario N5V 3N7
Phone: 519-451-9100
Fax: 519-451-6620
E-mail: rhocan@webgate.net
Page 106

St. Joesph's Health Care London
268 Grosvenor Street
P.O. Box 5777
London, Ontario N6A 4V2
Phone: 519-646-6100, extension 66034
Fax: 519-646-6215
E-mail: kathy.burrill@sjhc.london.on.ca
www.sjhc.london.on.ca
Pages 136-137

Spriet Associates
155 York Street
London, Ontario N6A 1A8
Phone: 519-672-4100
Fax: 519-433-9351
E-mail: mail@spriet.on.ca
www.spriet@on.ca
Page 128

The University of Western Ontario
1151 Richmond Street North
London, Ontario N6A 5B8
Phone: 519-661-2111
Fax: 519-661-3921
www.uwo.ca
Page 138

Western Fair Association
900 King Street
P.O. Box 7550
London, Ontario N5Y 5P8
Phone: 519-438-7203
Fax: 519-679-3124
E-mail: fair.info@westernfair.com
www.westernfair.com
Page 147

INDEX